SYSTEM DESIGN IN ONE EASY PIECE

Amazon Dynamo

Abdul Qadeer, Ph.D.

Systems Potpourri LLC

System Design in One Easy Piece: Amazon Dynamo

First Edition — June 2026
Volume 1 of the *System Design in One Easy Piece* series

Published by Systems Potpourri LLC
Wyoming, USA

Paperback ISBN: 979-8-9967654-2-3
Ebook (EPUB) ISBN: 979-8-9967654-0-9
PDF ISBN: 979-8-9967654-1-6

To the designers and engineers of Amazon Dynamo.

For showing the world that there is more than one right way to build a distributed system — and for having the courage to ship one of them.

Contents

Preface

Why This Book?

In the world of distributed systems, the Amazon Dynamo design (presented at SOSP 2007) is more than just a case study; it is a rite of passage. It was one of the first times a major tech giant pulled back the curtain and showed the world not just *how* to build a massive key-value store, but *why* they made the difficult trade-offs they did.

I wrote this book for three specific reasons.

First, **Dynamo is a complete curriculum in disguise.** If you truly understand Dynamo, you don't just understand a database; you understand the fundamental building blocks of modern distributed systems: Consistent Hashing, Versioning (Vector Clocks), Merkle Trees, Gossip Protocols, and Tunable Consistency (N, R, W). It is the perfect vessel for learning system design because it forces you to touch many parts of the stack.

Second, **I believe in First Principles over Rote Memorization.** As a professor, I often see students—and even experienced engineers—memorizing "tech stacks" or configuration flags without asking *why* they exist. They know how to configure a load balancer, but they cannot explain *why* we need a specific routing algorithm. This book takes a different approach. We do not just state that "Dynamo uses Version Vectors." We start from the problem (finding provenance in multiple replicas of a shopping cart), derive the necessity of happens-before relationship, and builds towards the solution. I want you to be able to re-derive these designs from scratch, not just remember them. This skill is invaluable for system design interviews as well.

Third, **the "Interview Gap."** As an observer of the industry, I have noticed that most system design interview resources treat these concepts superficially. They prioritize brevity over understanding. Candidates are taught to recite buzzwords like "gossip protocol" without understanding why a system would choose gossip over a central coordinator. This book aims to fix that. It offers the depth required for true engineering mastery, without forcing you to wade through hundreds of pages of fluff.

Why Dynamo in 2026?

In 2026, the software industry is fixated on Generative AI, Large Language Models, and Vector Databases. In this environment, revisiting a system from 2007 might seem like an exercise in history rather than engineering. However, the exact opposite is true.

The challenges that Amazon Dynamo solved—massive scale, high availability, and partition tolerance—are the exact challenges facing the infrastructure of the AI era. When we look under the hood of a modern Vector Database or a global inference cache, we do not find magic; we find Consistent Hashing, Gossip Protocols, Merkle Trees, and Quorum Consensus.

The syntax of our tools has changed, but the physics of distributed systems has not. This book dissects the Dynamo design not just to explain how key-value stores were built in the past, but to provide you with the immutable primitives you need to design the systems of the future. To master the architecture of 2026, one must first master the foundations laid by Dynamo.

What You Will Learn

A book is a promise to its reader, so let me be specific about mine. By the time you turn the final page of this volume, you will not just understand Amazon Dynamo as an artifact of the late 2000s — you will own a working mental model of the techniques that quietly run the large-scale systems you depend on every day. The table on the following page maps each problem Dynamo had to solve, the technique it pioneered or popularized in response, and — most importantly for your career as an engineer — where else you are likely to meet that same technique long after you have closed this book.

If one row in that table deserves a second glance, it is the seventh. Most working engineers have brushed up against Merkle trees somewhere — in Git's object store, in a Bitcoin block header, perhaps in IPFS (Inter Planetary File System) — but few have ever derived from first principles why the structure exists, or how it minimizes the bytes two replicas must exchange to discover their disagreements. Appendix A derives the structure from first principles, with worked shopping-cart examples; Merkle trees are a data structure well worth knowing in their own right.

A note on terminology while we are still in the preface. The Dynamo design refers to the per-object causality metadata as a vector clock. Strictly speaking, what Dynamo uses is a version vector — a close cousin of the vector clock that tracks causality among the replicas of a single object rather than among events in a process. The distinction is small but real, and we will draw that distinction carefully in Chapter 7. Throughout the rest of the book, we will write version vector when precision matters, and acknowledge vector clock as the more famous — if slightly looser — term you will encounter in interviews and in the original Dynamo design.

Table P.1 The distributed-systems curriculum hidden inside Dynamo.

Distributed Systems Problem	Technique You Will Master	Where Else You Will Meet It	Ch.
Why traditional ACID databases hit a wall at internet scale	The key-value model and the *BASE* alternative to *ACID*	Every NoSQL store; the state layer of modern microservices	1
Spreading data evenly across many machines, with no central master	Consistent Hashing and Virtual Nodes	CDNs, Memcached pools, sharded databases, modern L4/L7 load balancers	2
Cluster awareness without a single point of truth	Gossip protocols and implicit failure detection	Cassandra, Consul, HashiCorp Serf, blockchain peer-discovery layers	3
Surviving disk failure, machine death, and whole-datacenter outages	Replication with preference lists and rack-aware placement	Every replicated database, object store, and distributed file system	4
Tuning the consistency–availability dial on a per-request basis	Quorum Consensus with N, R, and W	Cassandra, Riak, and MongoDB read- and write-concern settings	5
Staying writable when "enough" replicas are down	Sloppy Quorum and Hinted Handoff	High-availability cache layers; multi-region active-active writes	5–6
Repairing replicas that have drifted badly apart	Anti-Entropy with **Merkle Trees** ★ bonus data structure	Git, Bitcoin, IPFS, ZFS, Cassandra repair	6, A
Detecting and resolving conflicting concurrent writes	Version Vectors and semantic reconciliation	Riak, CRDT-based systems, real-time collaborative editors	7, B
Hitting strict latency SLAs at the 99.9th percentile	Tail-latency engineering and zero-hop client routing	Every high-traffic API; modern service-mesh design	8
Knowing when to choose AP over CP — and being able to defend the choice	The CAP theorem applied, not just recited	Every system-design interview; any serious architectural review	1, 5, 10

How to Use This Book

This book is designed to take you from theory to practice. We will construct the architecture component by component, explaining the problem, the options, and the final design choice.

However, I respect that many of you are here for efficient review. For that reason, I have included a one-page capstone infographic — the **Dynamo Blueprint** (Figure 10.2, in Chapter 10) — at the end of the book. It distills the system's architecture and trade-offs into a single high-density reference, designed to refresh your memory on the critical diagrams minutes before an interview.

What I Ask of You

Writing a technical book is an iterative process, much like software itself. If you find value in these pages, or if you find a concept that could be explained more clearly, I want to hear from you.

The best way to reach me is on LinkedIn. I enjoy connecting with fellow engineers and students, and I often share updates on my future projects (including an upcoming deep dive on Load Balancers) there.

Connect with me here: linkedin.com/in/abdul-qadeer-15aab613

Enjoy the design process.

Abdul Qadeer, Ph.D.
June 2026

CHAPTER 1

The Shopping Cart Problem

Every successful product eventually grows faster than the system that was built to support it.

Amazon's e-commerce platform grew organically for years — more customers, more products, more orders. On a normal Tuesday, this growth is invisible to the engineering team. The database handles requests, writes complete, users get their confirmations. Everything works.

Then Black Friday arrives.

Millions of users arrive simultaneously, each hunting for deals. The traffic does not rise gradually; it arrives like a wave. And crucially, it concentrates. A single TV listed at a steep discount might attract tens of thousands of concurrent buyers. These are not independent users browsing independent pages. They are a thundering herd converging on the same rows, in the same tables, on the same database server. In distributed systems terminology, this is a hot spot — a point in the system where demand is orders of magnitude higher than the average.

Two engineering problems surface clearly in this environment. They are distinct in cause but connected in consequence.

The first is availability: any failure in the database — whether a network blip, a software bug, or a hardware fault — directly prevents customers from adding items to their shopping carts. Revenue stops the moment the database stops.

The second is scalability: under the thundering herd, the standard remedy of scaling up to a bigger server stops working, especially for traditional databases. Not gradually — it stops working, and past a certain threshold, begins working in reverse.

This chapter traces both problems from their roots and shows how they point toward a common solution: a key-value store that is always writable, horizontally scalable, and structurally simple.

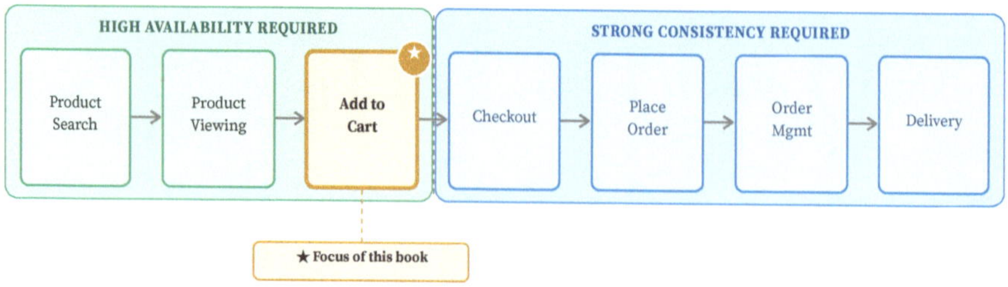

Figure 1.1 **The Customer's Buying Journey.** Two zones govern the entire flow: high availability from search through cart, strong consistency from checkout through delivery. A dropped "Add to Cart" click costs Amazon a sale. A double-charged payment costs a customer's trust. Different stakes demand different guarantees.

1.1 The Natural Starting Point: Relational Databases

When Amazon's shopping cart service was first built, reaching for a Relational Database Management System (RDBMS) was not a choice that needed justification. It was the default.

The relational model is extraordinarily mature. Its theoretical foundations date to Codd's 1970 paper. Decades of production use in banking, airline reservations, and retail have produced battle-tested implementations, well-understood failure modes, and a generation of engineers who think in tables, joins, and transactions. A shopping cart maps naturally onto a relational schema: a Users table, a Cart_Items table, a Products table. Foreign keys enforce referential integrity. Transactions ensure that a customer never sees a partially written cart.

As Figure 1.1 shows, the customer's journey has distinct phases with different requirements. Early in the journey — browsing products, building a cart — the operations are simple and the customer's tolerance for a refusal is essentially zero. A user who cannot add an item to their cart will not wait; they will leave. Later in the journey, at the moment of purchase, correctness becomes paramount: the system must know exactly how many units are in stock, and it must not sell the same unit twice.

The RDBMS handles all of these phases acceptably under normal load. The trouble begins when load stops being normal.

1.2 Two Trends That Emerge as You Grow

As a service like Amazon's cart grows — both organically through user acquisition and episodically through events like Black Friday — two distinct failure modes become visible. Neither is immediately obvious from a whiteboard design. Both require either production traffic or principled analysis to reveal.

1.2.1 Trend 1: The Availability Cliff

Databases fail. That is not a pessimistic assumption; it is an engineering baseline.

Jim Gray's foundational 1985 study, *Why Do Computers Stop and What Can Be Done About It?* (Tandem Technical Report TR-85.7), examined failure statistics from commercially deployed fault-tolerant systems. His finding was counterintuitive: hardware, the component most engineers worried about, was not the dominant cause of outages. Software failures and operator errors were. In the decades since, the landscape has shifted — cloud infrastructure has made hardware failure rarer — but the core lesson holds: **complex systems experience outages, and the causes are varied and often unpredictable.** Disk failures, network partitions, configuration errors, software bugs, planned maintenance windows, and cascading failures from dependent services all contribute.

> **Aside: The ACID Properties**
>
> Relational databases guarantee four properties for every transaction:
>
> - Atomicity: All operations in a transaction succeed or fail together. A half-written transaction is never visible.
> - Consistency: Every transaction moves the database from one valid state to another, respecting all defined rules and constraints.
> - Isolation: Concurrent transactions do not interfere with each other. The result is identical to running them one at a time.
> - Durability: Once a transaction is committed, it survives crashes, power failures, and restarts.
>
> These guarantees are genuinely powerful — and genuinely expensive. Enforcing them requires locks, logs, and coordination overhead that scales poorly under high concurrency write workloads. Under a network partition or hardware failure, simultaneously enforcing all four properties requires the database to reject writes rather than risk an inconsistent state — and that rejection is the availability cliff in action.
>
> Dynamo (and most of the NoSQL systems that followed it) trades

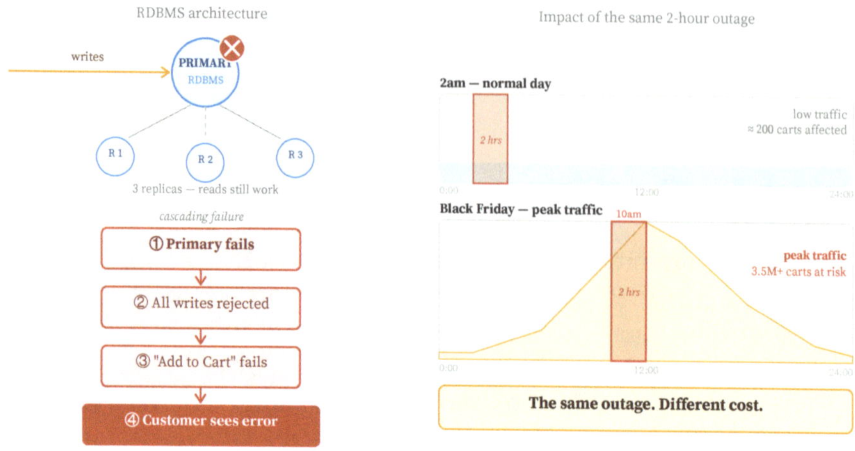

Figure 1.2 **The Availability Problem.** A single Primary failure cascades instantly: writes are rejected, “Add to Cart” breaks, and customers see an error page — even though three replicas remain healthy. The same two-hour outage at 2am on a usual day affects hundreds of users. During Black Friday peak it puts millions of carts at risk.

> these guarantees for the opposite philosophy, often labeled **BASE** — *Basically Available, Soft state, Eventually consistent*. The acronym was popularized by Dan Pritchett’s 2008 *ACM Queue* article “BASE: An ACID Alternative,” building on Eric Brewer’s CAP theorem; it is industry terminology that postdates Dynamo’s original 2007 design, which describes the system in its own words simply as “eventually consistent.” *Basically available* means the system keeps accepting reads and writes even when some replicas are unreachable. *Soft state* means a replica’s value can be temporarily stale, drifting toward correctness as updates propagate rather than changing atomically. *Eventually consistent* means that, given enough time without new writes, every replica converges on the same value.

For most of a service’s lifetime, these outages are invisible. A database that is available 99.9% of the time experiences about 8.7 hours of downtime per year. Spread across 365 days, no individual outage is long enough to make headlines.

Figure 1.2 captures the asymmetry: the same two-hour outage that is invisible at 2am on a usual day becomes a multi-million-cart disaster on Black Friday.

The financial impact of a shopping cart outage is acute and frontloaded. Unlike a reporting system or a data warehouse — where an hour of downtime means an hour of delayed analytics — a shopping cart outage means an hour of refused purchases. The Amazon Dynamo system (DeCandia et al., SOSP 2007) frames this directly: "even the slightest outage has significant financial consequences."

Why Replication Does Not Fully Solve This

The standard engineering response to availability concerns is replication: maintain multiple copies of the database so that if one fails, another can take over. For read operations, replication works well. For write operations under a network partition, it creates a dilemma with a name. See the following aside.

> **Aside: The CAP Theorem**
>
> In 2000, Eric Brewer formalized a fundamental constraint on distributed systems known as the *CAP theorem*. It states that a distributed data store cannot simultaneously guarantee all three of the following:
>
> - **Consistency (C):** Every read returns the most recent write. No node ever serves stale data.
> - **Availability (A):** Every request receives a response – not an error, not a timeout.
> - **Partition Tolerance (P):** The system keeps operating even when some nodes cannot communicate with each other due to a network failure.
>
> The uncomfortable truth for practitioners is that network partitions are not theoretical — they happen routinely in any large distributed system. A cable is cut. A switch misbehaves. A rack loses power momentarily. Because Partition Tolerance is therefore non-negotiable in practice, the real engineering choice reduces to a binary: **Consistency or Availability**. Traditional databases choose Consistency: they would rather reject your write than risk two nodes disagreeing. Amazon's Dynamo chooses Availability: it accepts every write, and reconciles any disagreements between nodes afterwards. One important precision: "Consistency" in CAP has a narrower meaning than in everyday conversation. It means every read, from any node, immediately reflects the latest write. Achieving this across hundreds of servers is expensive. Dynamo accepts a weaker form: your cart will be consistent *eventually*, just perhaps not in the next 200 milliseconds. We will build the machin-

> ery for this — quorums, version vectors, and anti-entropy — in the chapters that follow.

When an RDBMS is configured with *synchronous replication*, a network partition between the primary and its replicas creates an immediate choice: accept the write to the primary only (risking divergence) or reject the write entirely (preserving consistency). Traditional databases choose rejection. The result is that a network partition — not even a node failure, just a temporary loss of connectivity between nodes — causes write failures to propagate directly to the customer. The cart becomes read-only. Adding items is impossible until the partition heals.

Under normal conditions, partitions are brief enough to be invisible. Under Black Friday traffic, when load is highest and the probability of any component behaving abnormally is elevated, this is precisely the wrong moment for the system to become conservative about writes.

1.2.2 Trend 2: The Scalability Wall

The standard response to database performance problems is vertical scaling: buy a faster server with more cores, more RAM, and faster storage. For years, this works. Moore's Law ensures that each generation of hardware is meaningfully more capable than the last. The database team adds another core here, doubles the RAM there, and the system absorbs the growing load.

The critical question is: where does this trajectory end?

To find the ceiling, look at the largest instance available on any major cloud provider today: machines with close to 1,900 virtual CPUs and tens of terabytes of RAM are commercially available. These are extraordinary machines by any historical measure. They also represent a hard ceiling. Once your traffic requires more than one of these machines, vertical scaling is over. Horizontal scaling — distributing the workload across many machines — must take over.

But the transition is not smooth, because the RDBMS was not designed for it.

The Parallelism Limit of OLTP Workloads

The deeper problem is not the ceiling of a single machine; it is what happens as you approach that ceiling.

Online Transaction Processing (OLTP) workloads — the kind that power shopping carts — require **concurrency control**: a mechanism that ensures two concurrent writes to the same row do not corrupt each other's data. Locking is the classical implementation. When User A writes to a row, the database acquires a lock on that row. User B's write must wait until User A's transaction completes and the lock is released.

On a quiet Tuesday, locks are held for microseconds. The queue never builds. On Black Friday, with tens of thousands of users competing for the same product row, the lock queue grows faster than it drains. Adding more CPU cores does not help — more cores means more threads competing for the same lock, which increases contention, which increases the time each request spends waiting — driving up the latency the customer feels — and degrades throughput.

Aside: Amdahl's Law

In 1967, Gene Amdahl formalized a principle that constrains the speedup achievable by adding parallel processors to any computation that contains a serial component. If a fraction s of a program must execute serially (and cannot be parallelized), the maximum theoretical speedup from N processors is:

$$S(N) = \frac{1}{s + \frac{1-s}{N}}$$

As N $\to \infty$, the speedup approaches 1/s. If even 10% of the workload is serial, the maximum possible speedup — no matter how many processors you add — is 10$\times$.

The lock manager in an RDBMS is a serial bottleneck. Under high-contention workloads, the fraction of time threads spend waiting on locks grows as concurrency increases. Amdahl's Law ensures that adding cores past a certain point yields diminishing — and eventually negative — returns.

This is not a theoretical concern. Bang, May, Petrov, and Binnig ran an extensive empirical study on real multi-socket hardware with over 1,000 cores, published in *The Full Story of 1000 Cores* (VLDB Journal, 2022). Their conclusion is stark: **no concurrency control scheme can efficiently use large multi-socket hardware in a robust manner under high-conflict OLTP workloads.** Under the conditions that most resemble Black Friday hot-spot traffic — many threads competing for a small number of rows — throughput peaks early and then actively regresses as cores are added. The overhead of coordinating access across many cores exceeds the benefit of having more cores to do the work.

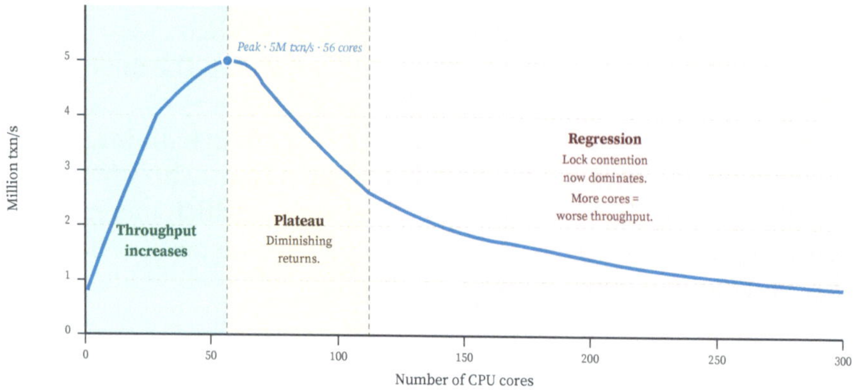

Curve traces TiCTOC (best-performing scheme on HPE hardware) · high-conflict TPC-C · Bang et al., VLDB 2022, Fig. 11. Traditional 2PL schemes (DL_DETECT, WAIT_DIE) peak lower and degrade faster. No scheme efficiently exploits 300+ cores.

Figure 1.3 **The Scalability Wall.** Even TICTOC — the best-performing concurrency control scheme — peaks at 5M txn/s around 56 cores and then declines under high-conflict TPC-C. Traditional lock-based schemes (DL_DETECT, WAIT_DIE) peak lower and degrade faster. See Bang et al., VLDB 2022, Fig. 11 for the full comparison across schemes and hardware platforms.

When Even Addition Becomes Hard: The Distributed Counter

The scalability limit revealed by the 1000 Cores paper is specific to concurrency control — to the machinery databases use to protect shared rows and its interactions with the underlying hardware. But the deeper problem is broader than locking. It is this: at sufficient scale, even operations with no inherent complexity become coordination problems.

Consider counting. Incrementing a number by one requires no joins, no transactions, no schema. It is the simplest write imaginable. Yet when a celebrity posts something and millions of followers react within seconds — from phones in Seoul, São Paulo, and Stockholm, hitting data centers on three continents simultaneously — that single increment becomes a distributed consensus problem. Netflix documented exactly this in their engineering blog (Netflix's Distributed Counter Abstraction, 2024): counting likes at global scale required a purpose-built distributed system with sharded counters, regional aggregation, and deliberate tradeoffs between accuracy and latency. The complexity did not come from the operation. It came from the coordination required to perform it simultaneously, everywhere, without a single point of serialization.

This is the underlying force that makes the shopping cart problem hard. The cart write is simple. The coordination across a distributed sys-

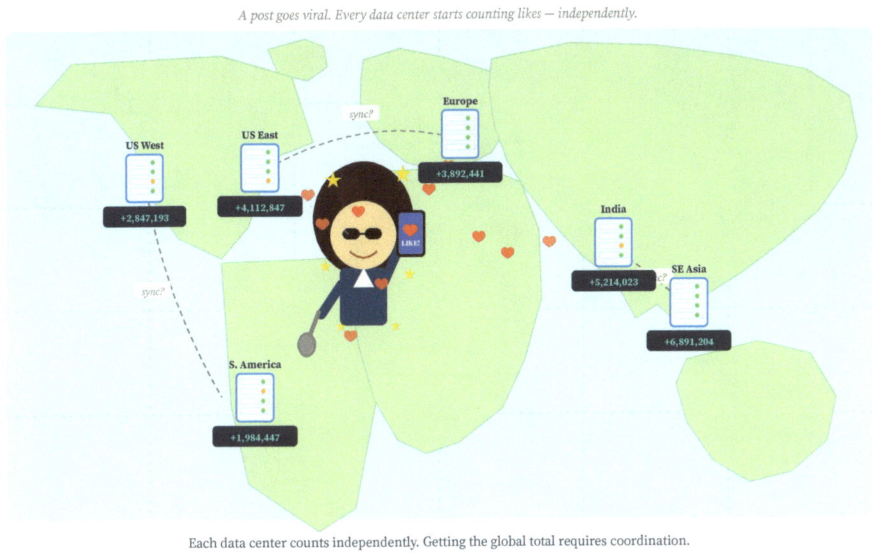

Figure 1.4 **When Counting Becomes a Global Problem.** A viral post reaches every data center simultaneously — each begins counting likes from zero, independently. Getting a single accurate global total requires every data center to synchronize its count, introducing exactly the coordination overhead Dynamo is designed to avoid.

tem is not.

1.3 Two Questions, One Direction

Both trends point toward the same question, approached from different angles.

The availability problem asks: **Can we afford to let the database's preference for consistency block writes to the shopping cart?** The cost of a rejected "Add to Cart" is immediate and measurable. The cost of a temporarily inconsistent cart — removing a deleted item from the cart a few seconds late — is survivable. A customer whose cart shows four items instead of three for one second will not notice. A customer whose "Add to Cart" click silently fails will.

The scalability problem asks: **Does the shopping cart actually need all of the machinery a relational database provides?** Transactions, foreign keys, joins, and multi-row consistency guarantees are powerful tools. They are also expensive ones. If the shopping cart workload does not actually require most of that machinery, then the cost is pure over-

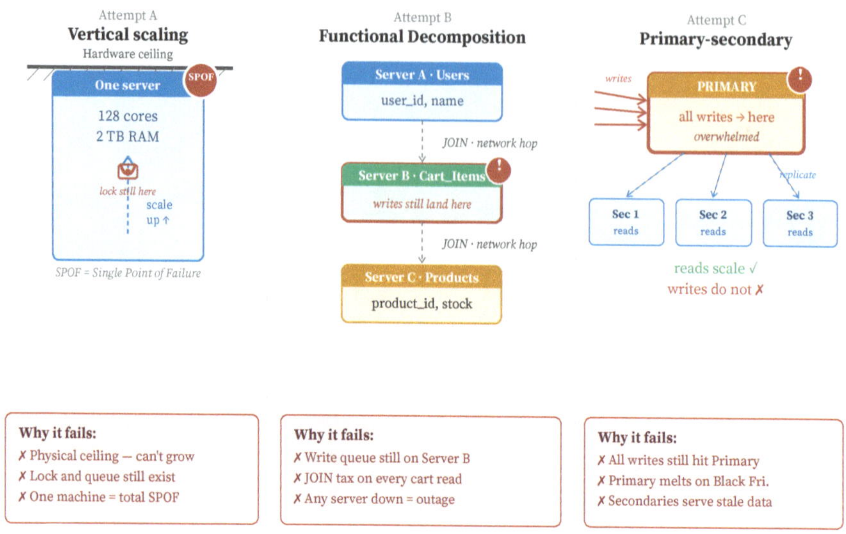

Figure 1.5 **Three Standard Responses, Three Dead Ends.** Vertical scaling hits a physical ceiling and leaves a single point of failure; functional decomposition (each table on a different server) moves the write bottleneck without eliminating it and makes any server failure a full outage; primary-secondary replication scales reads but every write still funnels to one node. None of the three addresses either the availability cliff or the scalability wall.

head.

The answer to both questions turns out to be the same insight, arrived at from opposite directions.

Amazon's own SLA for Dynamo required that 99.9% of all cart reads and writes complete within 300 milliseconds. That constraint — a P99.9 of 300ms — puts real pressure on any solution requiring cross-replica coordination on the write path: consensus protocols like Paxos or Raft can converge well within that budget, but doing so on every single write leaves little margin for hitting it consistently at scale.

1.4 The Insight: The Shopping Cart Is a Simple Workload

Look closely at what the "Add to Cart" operation actually requires.

A user adds an iPad to their cart. The database must record that this user's cart now contains this item. That is the entire operation. It does not require knowing what anyone else has in their cart. It does not require reading the Products table to check inventory — that check belongs at the moment of purchase, not at the moment of selection. It does not require

Table 1.1 Two use cases need different system architectures.

	Add to Cart	Place Order
Consistency need	Eventual	Immediate
Data touched	One user's cart	Inventory, payment, cart
Availability need	Must never fail	Can retry
Cross-row dependency	None	Yes (inventory count)

joining across multiple tables. It requires writing one piece of data that belongs to one user.

This is a point-access workload: one key (the user), one value (the cart contents). The relational model imposes structure — foreign keys, normalized tables, join relationships — that is genuinely valuable for complex queries but is pure overhead for a write that touches a single user's data and nothing else.

The "Add to Cart" operation and the "Place Order" operation are not the same problem wearing different clothes. They have fundamentally different requirements:

A system designed for "Place Order" — with full ACID transactions, inventory locking, and synchronous consistency — is the wrong tool for "Add to Cart." Using it anyway is like shipping every package in an armored truck because some packages contain valuables. It is far more efficient to only send valuable packages in an armored truck.

1.5 The Solution: Always Writable, Always Simple

The insight that the shopping cart is a point-access workload leads directly to a different data model.

Instead of treating the shopping cart as a set of rows distributed across three related tables, we treat the entire cart as a **single opaque object — a Key-Value pair**:

```
Key:   user_101_cart
Value: { "items": [{ "id": 42, "qty": 1 },
                   { "id": 87, "qty": 3 }],
         "ts": "2007-11-23T14:32:00Z" }
```

The entire cart — every item, every quantity, and a timestamp — lives in one blob, addressed by one key. Reading the cart requires no joins. Writing the cart requires no locks on other users' data. User 101's cart

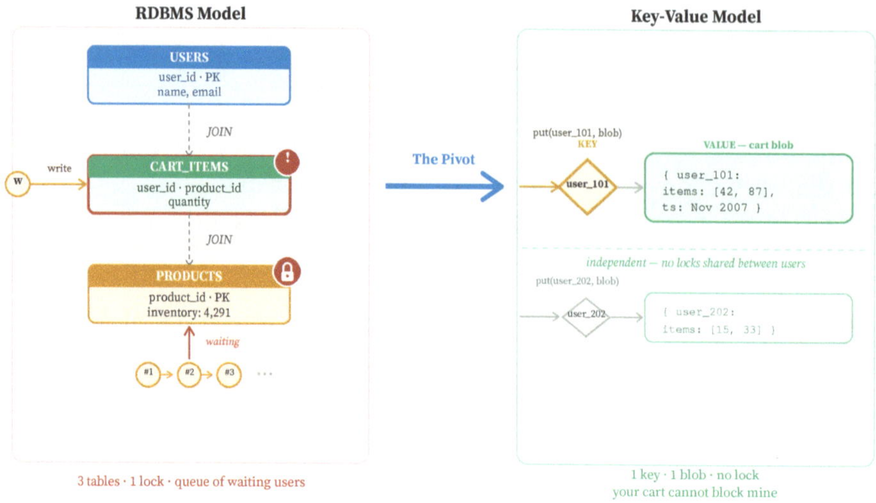

Figure 1.6 **The Key-Value Pivot.** Left: a write to Cart_Items requires two JOINs and a row lock on Products — every concurrent writer queues behind that one lock. Right: each user_id maps to a single independent blob. Two users writing simultaneously never touch the same key — no lock, no queue, no contention.

and User 102's cart are completely independent blobs; writing one cannot block the other, even under Black Friday load.

This model has two properties that directly address the two problems from earlier:

Availability: Because there are no cross-user dependencies, the system can accept a write to User 101's cart even when parts of the infrastructure are degraded. There is no inventory row to lock, no foreign key to validate. The write succeeds, and any consistency issues across replicas are resolved afterwards.

Scalability: Because each cart is independent of every other, carts can be distributed freely across many servers. User 101's cart lives on Server A; User 102's cart lives on Server Z. Neither server needs to know about the other for either write to succeed. This unlocks horizontal scaling: instead of one large server handling all writes, a hundred servers each handle a share.

The remaining question is mechanical: if we have a million carts and a hundred servers, how do we decide which cart goes to which server? And what happens when a server fails or a new one is added? A naive approach — assign carts by `hash(user_id) % number_of_servers` — breaks catastrophically every time the server count changes. Every cart would need to move. Adding a single server during a Black Friday traffic spike would require reshuffling roughly 99% of all data across the network — the worst possible moment for that operation.

We need a smarter algorithm. That algorithm is Consistent Hashing, and it is the subject of Chapter 2.

1.6 No Free Lunch

It is worth being explicit about what we have accepted in making this choice.

By designing a system that is always writable, we have accepted that two nodes might simultaneously accept conflicting writes to the same cart during a network partition. This can happen because each cart is replicated across multiple nodes, and Dynamo lets any reachable replica accept a write rather than first coordinating with the others; if a partition splits the cluster while a customer is updating their cart, two replicas on opposite sides of the split can each accept a different version of the same key, unaware of the other. When the partition heals, the system must detect the conflict and resolve it. This requires machinery — version vectors, quorum reads, anti-entropy — that we will build chapter by chapter.

We have also deliberately separated the shopping cart problem from the inventory problem. Inventory management — ensuring that we do not sell more units than exist — requires exactly the strong consistency that we have set aside for the cart. The solution is architectural: use a Dynamo-style store for the cart (where eventual consistency is acceptable), and use a separate, consistency-first service for the inventory check (invoked only at the moment of purchase). We will return to this distinction explicitly in the final chapter.

The design choices in this book are not presented as universally correct. They are presented as the right choices for a specific, well-defined problem: a write-heavy, point-access workload where availability takes precedence over immediate consistency. Different problems require different choices. Architecture is the art of matching tradeoffs to requirements.

In summary, we have decided to distribute shopping carts as key-value blobs across a cluster of servers. The next question is logistical: how do we decide, deterministically and efficiently, which server owns which cart? And how do we ensure that adding or removing a server does not require moving a huge amount of data?

The answer is *Consistent Hashing* — a simple technique that nonetheless underpins some of the largest storage systems in the world. That is the topic of our next chapter.

References

- *DeCandia et al., "Dynamo: Amazon's Highly Available Key-Value Store," ACM SOSP, 2007.*
- *Gray, J., "Why Do Computers Stop and What Can Be Done About It?", Tandem Technical Report TR-85.7, 1985.*
- *Bang, T., May, N., Petrov, I., Binnig, C., "The Full Story of 1000 Cores: An Examination of Concurrency Control on Real(ly) Large Multi-Socket Hardware," VLDB Journal, 2022.*
- *Shringi, R., Tkachuk, O., Sathyanarayanan, K., "Netflix's Distributed Counter Abstraction," Netflix Tech Blog, 2024.*
- *Brewer, E., "Towards Robust Distributed Systems," PODC Keynote, 2000.*
- *Amdahl, G., "Validity of the Single Processor Approach to Achieving Large Scale Computing Capabilities," AFIPS, 1967.*
- *Codd, E.F., "A Relational Model of Data for Large Shared Data Banks,"* Communications of the ACM, *Vol. 13, No. 6, pp. 377–387, June 1970.*

CHAPTER 2

The Ring (Partitioning)

In Chapter 1, we decided to store our shopping carts as key-value blobs. This buys us independence: User 101's cart has nothing to do with User 102's cart, so writing one can never block the other. But this decision immediately raises a logistics question: **where exactly do we put them?**

If you have 100 servers and 1 million shopping carts, you need a deterministic rule to decide which server holds which cart. The rule must work fast (every read and write depends on it), produce deterministic results (two different servers asked the same question must give the same answer), and handle servers joining or leaving without requiring a massive data shuffle.

A note before we start: this chapter leans on sidebars more than most. Consistent hashing has a small, simple core idea, but it accumulates a long tail of practical questions — why hash before the modulo, whether MD5 is safe to use, how the math behind the 1/N claim actually works — and each of those questions deserves a real answer rather than a handwave. We have pulled them out into asides so they do not interrupt the main thread. On a first read, feel free to skip every aside and follow only the numbered sections; the chapter's argument stands on its own without them. Come back for the asides on a second pass, or whenever a specific question is nagging at you.

2.1 The Trap of the Modulo Operator

The most natural rule is simple arithmetic. Take the hash of the key — to turn the string into a large integer — then divide by the number of servers and take the remainder.

With 10 servers:

- `hash("user_101") = 8450`
- `8450 % 10 = `**`0`**
- **Result:** Data goes to Server 0.

This rule is fast, deterministic, and trivial to implement. It works perfectly — until the number of servers changes.

2.1.1 Why this is a Disaster

Imagine Server 9 crashes, or you add an eleventh server to handle a traffic spike. The total server count changes from 10 to 11.

- `hash("user_101") = 8450`
- `8450 % 11 =` **`2`**
- **Result:** The data should now be on Server 2.

A single server change forces almost every key to a different server. If you have 10 servers and add one, roughly 10/11 $\approx$ 91% of all keys must be moved across the network. At 99 servers and one addition, the fraction approaches 99%. This is not a gradual migration — it is a simultaneous cascade of data transfers that can saturate your network and overwhelm every node in the cluster at exactly the moment you are trying to expand capacity.

We need a system where adding or removing a server displaces only a small fraction of the data — ideally around 1/N of the total, where N is the total server count in the system. There is a hashing mechanism with exactly that property and is called **Consistent Hashing**.

> **Aside: The Math Behind the Reshuffle**
>
> The claim that 90–99% of keys move when a server is added is mathematically precise, not an approximation. Under modulo hashing, a key k lands on server `hash(k) % N`. When N changes to N+1, a key stays on the same server only if `hash(k) % N == hash(k) % (N+1)`. For large random values of `hash(k)`, this occurs with probability approximately 1/(N+1). So the probability of a key **moving** is:
>
> $$P(\text{key moves}) = 1 - \frac{1}{N+1} = \frac{N}{N+1}$$
>
> | Servers before | Servers after | Keys that move |
> |---|---|---|
> | 9 | 10 | 90% |
> | 99 | 100 | 99% |
> | 999 | 1000 | 99.9% |
>
> As the cluster grows, the modulo operator becomes more brittle with every server addition.

> **Aside: Interview Question — Why Hash the Key First?**
>
> *Our cart IDs are auto-incrementing integers (1, 2, 3...). Why not use `cart_id % n_servers` directly? Why is the extra step of `hash(cart_id) % n_servers` necessary?*
>
> **The answer: to break patterns in the data.** In the real world, keys are rarely random. Sequential IDs like 10, 20, 30, 40 would all map to Server 0 under raw modulo — leaving all other servers idle. This is called **data skew**, and it creates a hot spot that no amount of additional hardware can fix. A hash function acts like a blender. It takes predictable inputs (10, 20, 30) and produces outputs that are statistically indistinguishable from random numbers, scattering them uniformly across all servers regardless of the input pattern. This question tests whether you understand *why* we hash, not just *that* we hash. Many candidates memorize the step without being able to explain it.

2.1.2 When You Need Locality: Range Queries and Composite Keys

Hashing is powerful precisely because it destroys order. That strength is also its central limitation.

The scenario: you need to retrieve all of a user's orders from July 2025. Under consistent hashing:

- `hash("order_july_1")` might land on Node A.
- `hash("order_july_2")` might land on Node D.
- `hash("order_july_3")` might land on Node B.

To fetch all July orders, you may need to query every node in the cluster. This is called a **scatter-gather query**, and it is expensive.

Order-preserving partitioning solves this by treating the key space like a sorted dictionary rather than a hash map. You assign *ranges* of raw key values to servers:

- Node A handles keys [A–K]
- Node B handles keys [L–Z]
- Node C handles keys [0–500]

Keys that are numerically or lexicographically close land on the same node, making range queries fast and cheap. But this approach reintroduces the skew problem from a different angle: if your keys are timestamps, every new write lands on the node handling "today," while all nodes handling "last month" sit idle.

Table 2.1 The composite key divides responsibility between two parts.

Part	Role	Hashed?
Partition key	Determines *which server*	Yes — ensures even distribution
Sort key	Determines *order within that server*	No — preserves local ordering

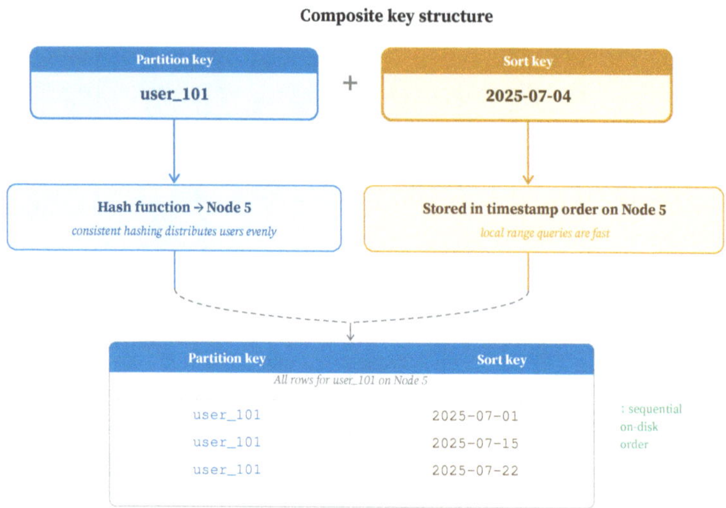

Figure 2.1 **The Composite Key Structure.** The partition key (hashed) determines which node holds the record; the sort key (unhashed) preserves order within that node — the approach DynamoDB and Cassandra use to trade fast global range queries for fast local ones.

You have traded bad range queries for bad load balancing.

The composite key: the best of both worlds. Modern systems like DynamoDB and Cassandra resolve this with a two-part key:

With a composite key of (user_id, timestamp), the system hashes user_id to find the correct server, then stores all of that user's records in timestamp order on that server. You can answer "all orders by User A in July" with a single-node range scan. You cannot answer "all orders from all users on July 4" without hitting every node — that remains a scatter-gather query.

The rule of thumb for choosing your partitioning scheme:

- Need global range queries ("all orders from everyone on July 4") → **order-preserving partitioning** (Google Bigtable, Apache HBase). Accept the hot-spot risk.

- Need local range queries ("all orders for User A in July") → **composite keys with consistent hashing** (DynamoDB, Cassandra).
- Need only point lookups ("the cart for user_101") → **consistent hashing** (Dynamo). This is the model we use for the rest of this book.

The interview question "what if your workload needs range queries?" now has a concrete, structured answer.

2.1.3 Summary of Partitioning Approaches

Table 2.2 Summary of partitioning approaches.

Approach	**Even load?**	**Range queries?**	**Graceful changes?**
Modulo hashing	Yes, if keys are random	No	No — massive reshuffle
Order-preserving partitioning	Only if keys are uniform	Yes, global	Yes
Consistent hashing	Yes	Local only (composite keys)	Yes, ~1/N moves

2.2 Visualizing the Ring

Consistent hashing maps both servers and data keys onto the same space — a circular ring — so that server additions and removals only affect nearby data.

Imagine the output space of our hash function (MD5 produces 128-bit integers) not as a straight line from 0 to $2^{128}-1$, but as a circle. The largest value wraps around to 0, like a clock face. The top is 0; going clockwise takes you all the way to $2^{128}-1$, and one step further brings you back to 0.

2.2.1 Step A: Place the Servers

We can hash the IP address (or hostname) of each physical server to find its position on the ring. The result is pseudo-random but deterministic: the same IP always produces the same position. Dynamo used a simpler strategy of picking a position on the ring randomly whenever a new server joins (let's call it strategy 1 for comparison purposes with other strategies which we'll formalize in §2.5).

- Server A hashes to position **12:00.**
- Server B hashes to position **4:00.**
- Server C hashes to position **8:00.**

Each server now "owns" the arc between itself and its predecessor, walking clockwise:

- Server A owns **(8:00, 12:00]** — everything after Server C's position, up to and including Server A's.
- Server B owns **(12:00, 4:00]**.
- Server C owns **(4:00, 8:00]**.

The notation (8:00, 12:00] means: the position 8:00 is not included (it belongs to Server C), but 12:00 is included (it belongs to Server A). A key that hashes to exactly a server's position belongs to that server.

2.2.2 Step B: Place the Data

We hash the key user_101 to find its position on the ring. Suppose it lands at 2:00. We use the same hash function that we used to find the location of a server. Therefore, like a server, a hash key can land anywhere on the ring.

2.2.3 Step C: The Clockwise Walk

To find which server owns a given key, we apply one rule: walk clockwise from the key's position until you hit a server.

user_101 is at 2:00.

Walking clockwise, the first server we hit is Server B at 4:00.

Verdict: Server B owns this shopping cart.

Every node in the cluster can apply this rule independently using only the list of known server positions — no central coordinator needed.

2.2.4 Why this solves the "Modulo Problem"

Now imagine we introduce Server D at position 2:00, inserted between Server A (12:00) and Server B (4:00).

Before Server D's arrival:

Server B owned (12:00, 4:00] — a two-hour arc on the clock face.

After Server D joins at 2:00:

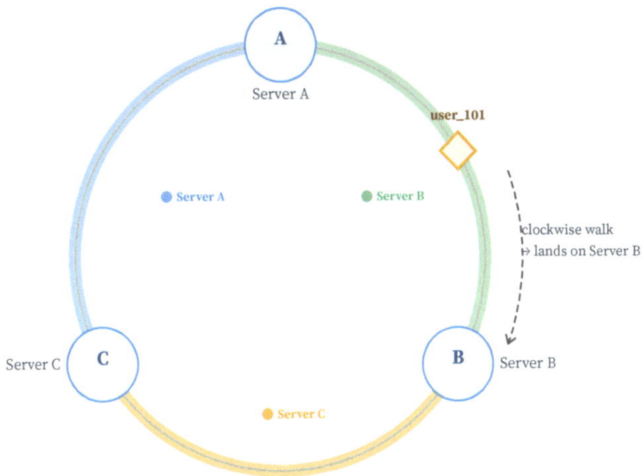

Figure 2.2 **The Basic Consistent Hashing Ring.** Servers and keys share the same circular hash space; a key is owned by the first server encountered walking clockwise from its position — here, user_101 at 2:00 lands on Server B.

Server D now owns (12:00, 2:00] — taken from the front of Server B's old range.

Server B now owns (2:00, 4:00] — its remaining portion.

Servers A and C are completely unaffected. Their arcs did not change.

Only the keys in the range (12:00, 2:00] need to move from Server B to Server D. In a balanced ring with N servers, adding one new server displaces approximately 1/(N+1) of all data, which simplifies to roughly 1/N for large N.

Compare this to the modulo operator: adding Server D under modulo rules forces a recalculation of `hash(key) % N` for every single key in the system — roughly 91% of all data must move. Under consistent hashing, only the keys in Server D's new arc change hands. Every other key stays exactly where it was.

> ### Aside: The Formal Proof That Only 1/N Keys Move
>
> *For readers who want to verify the claim with a derivation.* Let K be the total number of keys and N the number of servers. In consistent hashing, each server owns roughly 1/N of the ring and thus 1/N of all keys on average.

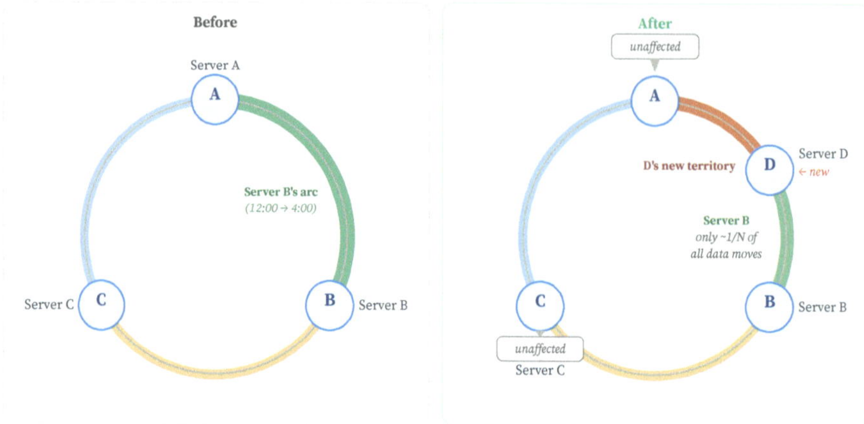

Figure 2.3 **Adding a Server: Only 1/N Data Moves.** Before: Server B owns the full arc from 12:00 to 4:00. After: Server D joins at 2:00 and takes only the front portion of that arc — Servers A and C are completely unaffected.

Adding one new server (total: N+1): The new server lands at a random position on the ring, inside one existing server's arc. It takes the keys in its portion of that arc — roughly 1/(N+1) of all keys — and every other server is untouched. **Total data moved ≈ 1/(N+1) ≈ 1/N for large N.**

A common point of confusion: why isn't it 1/(2N)? One might expect the new server to take exactly half of its predecessor's range. But the new server does not take half of one server's range — it takes enough to reach its own fair share of 1/(N+1) of the total data. If the predecessor had more than its fair share (due to uneven random placement), the new server takes correspondingly more. On average, the total that moves is 1/(N+1), not 1/(2N).

Comparison:

Event	Modulo hashing	Consistent hashing
Add 1 server (10→11)	~91% of keys move	~9% of keys move
Add 1 server (99→100)	~99% of keys move	~1% of keys move

Aside: MD5 Deep Dive

How to Use a Hash Function in Practice. In code, you almost always work with the hash output as a large integer, not a hex string, because you need to do arithmetic on it (place it on the ring, compare positions). Here is how to convert in two common environments.

Python:

```
import hashlib
key = "user_101"
hash_hex = hashlib.md5(key.encode()).hexdigest()
hash_int = int(hash_hex, 16)      # convert hex -> integer
ring_position = hash_int % (2**128)
```

Shell (Bash):

```
echo -n "user_101" | md5sum \
  | awk '{print "0x"$1}' | xargs printf "%d\n"
```

The result is a large integer in the range $[0, 2^{128})$ that you use for position comparisons on the ring.

Is MD5 Safe to Use for Ring Placement? MD5 is cryptographically broken — it is computationally feasible to find two inputs that produce the same hash output (a collision). For password storage or digital signatures, this is a fatal weakness. For ring placement, it is irrelevant. A collision in our context means two different keys hash to the same ring position — the same server handles both. The consequence: one server handles two carts instead of one. The system stays up; no data is stolen or corrupted. MD5 also computes faster than SHA-256, which matters when a node is hashing millions of requests per second. This is why Dynamo itself uses MD5 for key placement. Cassandra defaults to MurmurHash (Murmur3) and Riak to SHA-1 — both chosen for speed and uniform distribution rather than cryptographic strength.

The rule: use a cryptographic hash for *protection* (passwords, signatures). Use MD5 or MurmurHash for *placement* (routing, load balancing).

Why MD5 Distributes Uniformly — The Avalanche Effect. How do we know MD5 will scatter keys evenly around the ring, and not cluster them? The answer is the **Avalanche Effect**: changing a single bit of the input flips approximately 50% of the output bits, ensuring that similar inputs produce wildly different outputs. A demonstration with sequential cart IDs:

Input	MD5 (first 8 hex chars)	Position (% 10)
user_1	c4ca4238	8
user_2	c81e728d	3
user_3	eccbc87e	4
user_4	a87ff679	9

Sequential inputs (1, 2, 3, 4) produce positions (8, 3, 4, 9) — statistically indistinguishable from random selection. No deterministic function can be proven perfectly random, but the Avalanche Effect makes MD5's output practically uniform for load-balancing purposes, with no special treatment needed for sequential or patterned keys.

2.2.5 Summary

Consistent hashing maps both servers and keys onto the same circular space. Finding the owner of a key requires only a clockwise walk to the nearest server. Adding or removing a server moves only the keys in the affected arc — roughly 1/N of the total — and leaves the rest of the cluster undisturbed. This property is called the **Clockwise Rule**, and it reappears in Chapter 4 (building the preference list for replication) and Chapter 5 (extending the walk for sloppy quorum).

2.3 The "Heavy Neighbor" Problem

The theory of consistent hashing is elegant, but the real world introduces a practical flaw.

Hash functions are pseudo-random. There is no guarantee that servers will land at evenly spaced positions on the ring. Imagine three servers — Server X, Server Y, and Server Z — where the hash function places them at 12:00, 1:00, and 2:00 respectively.

The consequences of this clustering:

- Server Y owns only the arc **(12:00, 1:00]** — a tiny sliver.
- Server Z owns only the arc **(1:00, 2:00]** — another tiny sliver.
- **Server X owns the arc (2:00, 12:00]** — approximately 83% of the entire ring.

Server X absorbs 83% of all traffic while Y and Z sit nearly idle. Furthermore, not all servers are equal. If Server Z is a powerful 64-core machine but Server X is an older 4-core machine, our ring can assign them equal shares regardless of capacity — so the weakest server gets the most work.

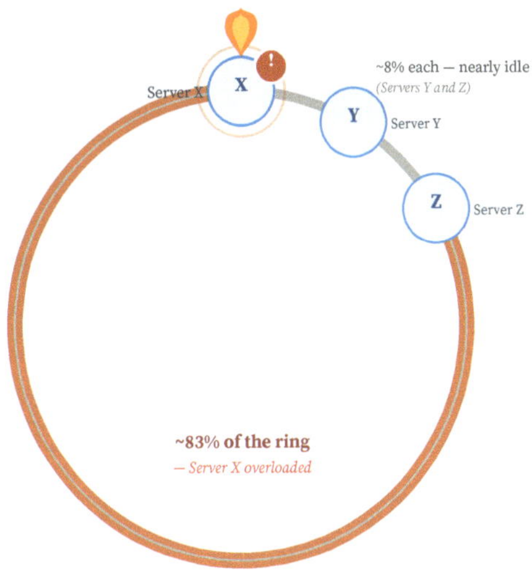

Figure 2.4 **The Heavy Neighbor Problem.** Pseudo-random placement clusters Servers X, Y, and Z tightly together on the ring (at 12:00, 1:00, and 2:00), so Server X inherits roughly 83% of all traffic while Y and Z sit nearly idle.

2.4 The Solution: Virtual Nodes (V-Nodes)

The fix is to stop mapping one physical server to one point on the ring. Instead, we map each physical server to **many** points. These are called **Virtual Nodes** (or V-Nodes, or tokens).

- Server A (physical) becomes tokens: $A_1, A_2, A_3, \ldots, A_{100}$
- Server B (physical) becomes tokens: $B_1, B_2, B_3, \ldots, B_{100}$
- Server C (physical) becomes tokens: $C_1, C_2, C_3, \ldots, C_{200}$ *(twice as many, because Server C is twice as powerful)*

We scatter these tokens randomly across the ring as if each were an independent server. A key still uses the Clockwise Rule to find its owning token — but that token maps back to a physical server.

> ### Aside: Creating Virtual Nodes — The Recipe
>
> Virtual nodes can be created by hashing *synthetic names* — the server's IP combined with a numeric index:
>
> ```
> import hashlib
> def vnode_position(ip: str, index: int) -> int:
> ```

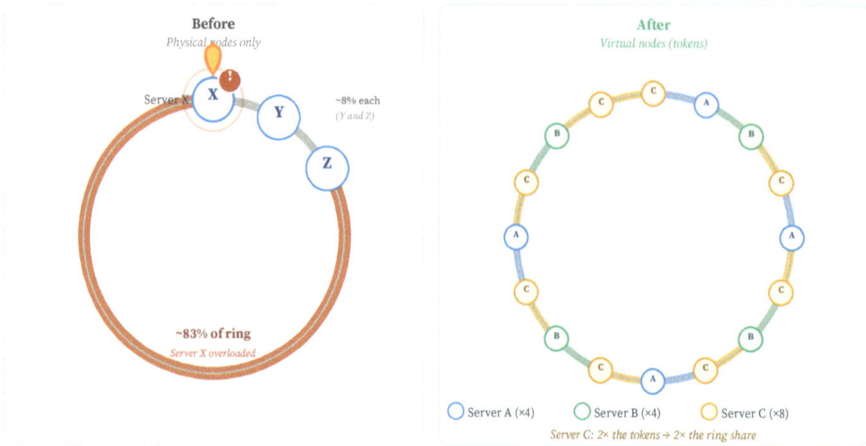

Figure 2.5 **Virtual Nodes: Before and After.** Replacing each physical server with many scattered tokens averages away the heavy-neighbor clustering from Figure 2.4 — and lets a more powerful server (Server C, with twice the tokens) claim a proportionally larger share of the ring.

```
    synthetic_name = f"{ip}#{index}"
    hash_hex = hashlib.md5(synthetic_name.encode()).hexdigest()
    return int(hash_hex, 16)
# Server 192.168.1.5 gets 100 virtual nodes
server_ip = "192.168.1.5"
positions = [vnode_position(server_ip, i) for i in range(100)]
```

Each call produces a distinct position on the ring. Together, the 100 positions of Server A scatter across the ring as if 100 independent servers were present — but they all route traffic to the same physical machine. Had we used Dynamo's strategy 1, finding the ring location would have been as simple as generating a random number. Though in that case each node (or virtual node) will need to persist its location and will need to disseminate this information to others (a topic of our later chapters).

2.4.1 The Magic of Mixing

With many virtual nodes per physical server, the clustering problem resolves itself statistically. Imagine 100 virtual nodes per physical server across three machines — 300 tokens scattered pseudo-randomly across the ring. The laws of large numbers ensure that each physical server ends up owning approximately **equal shares** of the ring, regardless of where the physical servers happened to land.

Three properties emerge from this design:

Uniform load distribution. Each physical server holds many small, scattered arcs rather than one large continuous arc. The heavy-neighbor problem averages away at scale.

Graceful failure. If Server A fails, its 100 token positions are each inherited by whichever server is clockwise-next in that neighborhood. No single server absorbs a "double load" — the extra traffic is distributed across many survivors.

Capacity-proportional assignment. A server that is twice as powerful receives twice as many tokens and therefore owns approximately twice the share of the ring. In our example, Server C with 200 tokens handles twice the traffic of Servers A and B with 100 each.

Note that this proportionality assumes read/write traffic is roughly proportional to the number of keys stored on a node. For workloads where a small number of "hot keys" receive a disproportionate share of requests — viral content, trending products — additional strategies such as request-level sharding or a dedicated cache layer may be needed. We address this case when we discuss tail latency in Chapter 8.

2.5 Evolution of the Placement Strategy

The virtual node design described above — each physical server assigned random token positions — was Dynamo's original production deployment. It works, but Amazon's engineers discovered three operational problems that motivated two rounds of refinement (slow bootstrapping, costly Merkle tree invalidation, and difficult archiving — each detailed shortly).

Understanding this evolution matters for two reasons. First, Strategy 3 is what Dynamo actually runs in production — the system this book is about. Second, Chapters 3 and 4 make explicit references to the differences between strategies, particularly in how gossip protocol payloads differ and how the preference list is constructed. We need all three strategies defined here before those references make sense.

The core problem with random token placement is that it couples two concerns that should be independent: **where data lives** (partitioning) and **which node is responsible for it** (placement). Every change to the ring topology forces a data redistribution. The three strategies progressively decouple these concerns.

2.5.1 Strategy 1: Random Tokens, Variable Ranges (Original Dynamo)

In Strategy 1, each node is assigned T tokens chosen uniformly at random from the 128-bit hash space. The tokens of all nodes are sorted by value; consecutive token pairs define the key ranges. Each node's token positions determine both its place on the ring and which keys it owns.

The three problems Amazon encountered in production:

Problem 1 — Slow bootstrapping. When a new node joins the ring at a random position, it takes a portion of an existing node's key range. Because range boundaries are arbitrary (determined by where random tokens landed), the existing node cannot copy a file. It must scan its entire local database row by row, checking each key's hash to determine whether it falls in the range to be handed off. On a production node handling millions of requests per day, this background scan competes with live traffic. During peak shopping seasons, bootstrapping a new node under Strategy 1 took close to a day.

Problem 2 — Merkle tree invalidation. Every time a node joins or leaves the ring, the key ranges change. Each range has an associated Merkle tree used for replica synchronization (covered in Chapter 6). When a range boundary shifts, the Merkle tree for that range must be recalculated from scratch — a non-trivial computation on a busy system.

Problem 3 — Difficult archiving. It is tempting to think this is solved by simply asking each node for its data in turn, but the real difficulty is not the asking — it is knowing what you got. Under Strategy 1 there is no fixed, enumerable list of ranges to check off as "done." A node's range boundaries are just whatever its neighbors' random tokens happen to be at that exact moment, and on a live hundred-node cluster, membership keeps changing while the backup is running: nodes join, leave, and rebalance over the hours a full snapshot takes. If a range boundary shifts between the time you snapshot Node 7 and the time you snapshot its neighbor, a key can fall through the seam and be missed entirely, or get captured by both and show up twice — and because there is no fixed manifest of ranges to diff against, you cannot even detect that this happened. A failed or restarted backup has no clean checkpoint to resume from either; you are back to asking every node again. Taking a full-cluster snapshot under Strategy 1 means retrieving keys from each node separately and reassembling them against a constantly shifting set of boundaries — an operationally fragile process precisely because there is nothing stable to verify completeness against.

The root cause: partitioning and placement are intertwined. To fix one, you disrupt the other.

2.5.2 Strategy 2: Fixed Partitions, Random Tokens

Strategy 2 decouples the partitioning from the placement by pre-cutting the ring into Q fixed, equal-sized partitions — before any server is assigned.

A concrete numerical example:

Suppose Q = 12 (twelve partitions) and S = 3 servers. Each partition spans exactly 1/12 of the 128-bit hash space:

- Partition 0: hash values $[0, 2^{128}/12)$
- Partition 1: hash values $[2^{128}/12, 2 \times 2^{128}/12)$
- ...
- Partition 11: hash values $[11 \times 2^{128}/12, 2^{128})$

Nodes are still assigned T random tokens, but the tokens now only determine *routing* — for each partition, you walk clockwise from the end of that partition and find whichever node's token is the first one you reach. That node owns the partition. The partition boundaries themselves are fixed and never change.

This raises a natural question: what if two nodes happen to have tokens landing close together, right next to a partition boundary? There is no ambiguity here, even so. The rule is still simply "walk clockwise from the boundary and stop at the first token you reach"; whichever node owns that token owns the partition, regardless of how close the next-nearest token happens to be. Two tokens being close together only means the wedge of ring *between* them is small — it does not blur which node a given partition boundary resolves to.

With Q = 12 and S = 3, each server handles roughly 4 partitions on average.

What this fixes:

- **Bootstrapping:** a new node takes over whole partitions. "Hand off Partition 4" means copying a single bounded file — no row-by-row scan.
- **Merkle trees:** each Merkle tree covers a fixed partition. When a partition moves, its Merkle tree travels with it — no recalculation.
- **Archiving:** the complete dataset is exactly 12 partition files — a clean, enumerable set.

What remains: nodes still hold T random tokens, so the number of partitions assigned to each node can vary. A node that happens to hold more tokens ends up responsible for more partitions, which can create load imbalance in small clusters. The reason for holding more tokens is that the token still controls routing, so a node at the center of a dense cluster of token positions will be the nearest clockwise neighbor for more partition boundaries.

2.5.3 Strategy 3: Fixed Partitions, Proportional Tokens (What Dynamo Uses)

Strategy 3 takes Strategy 2's fixed partitions and adds one more constraint: instead of T random tokens per node, each node holds exactly **Q/S tokens** — where Q is the total number of partitions and S is the current number of nodes.

This guarantees that every node handles the same number of partitions, producing uniform load distribution by construction rather than by statistical luck.

A concrete example:

With Q = 12 and S = 3, each node holds Q/S = 4 tokens. The tokens are assigned so that each node's 4 partitions are evenly distributed around the ring rather than clustered.

How ring changes work under Strategy 3:

- **A node leaves the ring:** its 4 tokens are distributed one-by-one to the remaining 2 nodes (each absorbs 2), preserving the Q/S balance. Each receiving node gains one whole partition — a clean file copy.
- **A node joins the ring:** it "steals" Q/S tokens (12/4 = 3) from the existing nodes — taking one token from each — until it holds 3 partitions. Again, whole partitions move; no arbitrary boundary scans.

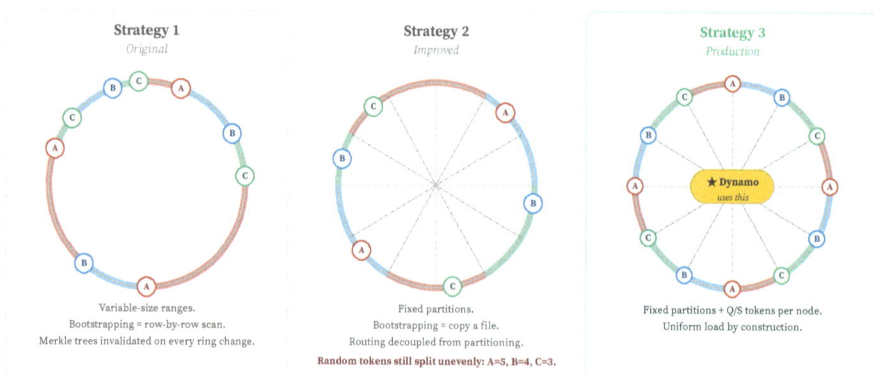

Figure 2.6 **The Three Partitioning Strategies.** Dynamo evolved through three strategies in production — Strategy 3, with fixed partitions and proportional tokens, is what shipped.

Dynamo currently uses Strategy 3.

For the remainder of this book, when we refer to the partitioning scheme, we mean Strategy 3 unless otherwise noted. The gossip payloads in Chapter 3, the preference list construction in Chapter 4, and the anti-entropy protocol in Chapter 6 are all designed with Strategy 3's clean partition boundaries in mind.

Aside: The Paradox of "Uniform" Randomness — Why Randomness Alone Is Not Enough

You might ask: we chose MD5 specifically because its Avalanche Effect produces uniform output. So why do we need fixed partitions at all? If the hash is uniform, shouldn't the server spacing be perfect?

The answer is the classic conflict between **probability and geometry**. MD5 ensures that *keys* — millions of them — are uniformly spread across the hash space. But *nodes* are few in number. When you place a small number of points randomly on a circle, the Birthday Paradox and basic probability guarantee clustering: some nodes will land close together (creating small, lightly loaded arcs) and some will be far apart (creating large, heavily loaded arcs). The smaller the number of nodes, the worse this effect. The Birthday Paradox says that with N random points on a circle, the expected minimum gap between two points is proportional to $1/N^2$. That means clustering of points is statistically inevitable.

To convince yourself, you can run a quick simulation: scatter points randomly on a ring of size 10,000 and see how they cluster. We did exactly that, and the two scenarios below show the result. On the left, 10 points are placed randomly on the ring — clustering is already visible, and the red pair marks the smallest gap. On the right, 200 points are placed on the same ring; there are now many small clusters, but overall the points are spread out far more uniformly.

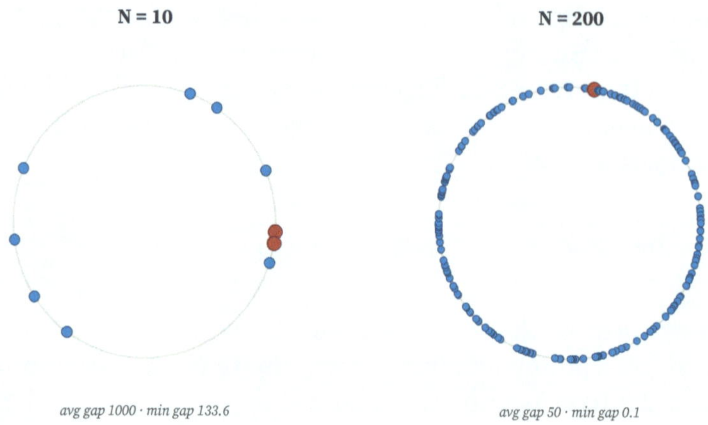

That happens due to a phenomenon called the law of large numbers in probability theory. When N (the number of things we put on the ring) is relatively small, clustering happens — we dealt with this for our servers using many virtual nodes per physical server and Strategy 3. When N is large, as with the incoming key traffic — likely millions or even billions of puts and gets per day — those keys are expected to be uniformly distributed over the ring.
Strategy 3 solves this not by using a better random number generator, but by abandoning randomness for node spacing altogether. Partitions are fixed by design; token assignments are controlled. The geometry is enforced, not hoped for.

A natural concern is that the Q/S formula breaks down when S does not divide Q evenly — a 7-server cluster with Q = 120 gives 120/7 = 17.14, not a whole number. The fix is to remember that S counts virtual nodes, not physical servers. Because you control how many virtual nodes each physical server receives, you can nudge the total virtual node count to the nearest divisor of Q whenever a new physical server joins. With Q = 120, the valid values of S are its divisors: 8, 10, 12, 15, 20, and so on. When a 7th physical server joins a 6-server cluster, you assign it slightly fewer virtual nodes than its peers, targeting the next clean divisor rather than a naive equal split. The imbalance this creates — one server carrying one or two fewer partitions than the others — is a small, deliberate tuning decision made once at join time, not a structural flaw in the scheme. Virtual nodes turn S from a fixed constraint into an adjustable knob, and that is precisely why Strategy 3 works smoothly in practice across a wide range of cluster sizes.

2.6 Summary

By using **Consistent Hashing** with **Virtual Nodes** and the production-proven **Strategy 3** partitioning scheme, we have turned our cluster into an elastic resource:

- Adding a node displaces only ~1/N of the data — the keys in the new node's partitions.
- Removing a node redistributes only its Q/S partitions, whole files at a time, with no boundary scans.
- Heterogeneous hardware is accommodated by assigning more tokens to more powerful machines.
- Bootstrapping is fast, Merkle tree maintenance is cheap, and full-cluster archiving is a clean enumeration of Q partition files.

But the ring raises an immediate practical question: how does Server A know that Server B exists? How does it learn Server B's IP address, its token positions, or whether Server B is currently alive?

In a five-node cluster, you could hardcode this information. In a thousand-node cluster where hardware fails daily and capacity is added automatically, a static configuration file is impossible. We need a mechanism by which thousands of nodes stay synchronized about cluster membership — without a central coordinator.

That mechanism is the **Gossip Protocol**, and it is the subject of Chapter 3.

References

- *DeCandia et al., "Dynamo: Amazon's Highly Available Key-Value Store," ACM SOSP, 2007. §4.1 (Partitioning Algorithm), §4.2 (Virtual Nodes), §6.2 (Ensuring Uniform Load Distribution).*
- *Karger, D., Lehman, E., Leighton, T., Panigrahy, R., Levine, M., Lewin, D., "Consistent Hashing and Random Trees: Distributed Caching Protocols for Relieving Hot Spots on the World Wide Web," ACM STOC, 1997.*
- *Stoica, I., Morris, R., Karger, D., Kaashoek, M. F., Balakrishnan, H., "Chord: A Scalable Peer-to-peer Lookup Service for Internet Applications," ACM SIGCOMM, 2001.*

CHAPTER 3

The Nervous System (Gossip Protocol)

In Chapter 2, we built the Ring. We established that to find a specific shopping cart—say, `user_101`—you hash the key, locate its position on the ring, and route the request to the server responsible for that arc. Call it Server B.

But this assumes a massive piece of magic: The Map.

To route a request to Server B, the routing node needs to know that Server B exists, what Server B's IP address is, and which portion of the key-space Server B is responsible for. In a cluster of five nodes, you can hardcode this information in a configuration file. In a cluster of a thousand nodes, where hardware fails daily and capacity scales automatically, a static file is impossible.

We need a mechanism that keeps thousands of nodes synchronized about cluster membership state—without any central coordinator.

3.1 What Every Node Needs to Know

Before solving the synchronization problem, we should be precise about what information each node needs. There are three distinct pieces:

- **Identity:** The IP addresses (or hostnames) of every other node in the cluster and ring.
- **Liveness:** Which of those nodes are currently alive and reachable.
- **Ring Ownership:** Which token ranges or partitions each node is responsible for.

The third item deserves particular attention. Both partitioning strategies (Strategy 1 and Strategy 3) require gossip to distribute ring ownership information—the strategies differ in what they gossip and how each node derives topology from what it receives.

Under **Strategy 1** (random tokens), each node selects a random token position when it joins and gossips that position to its peers. Once a node has accumulated the token positions of all other nodes through gossip, it can derive the complete ring topology—its predecessor, its successor, its key range boundaries—by sorting the accumulated token list. The gossip payload is compact: just an (identity, token position) pair per node. But the distributed state is essential: a new node cannot determine where its key range begins or know which existing node to contact to claim its portion of the ring, without first receiving other nodes' token positions through gossip.

Under **Strategy 3** (fixed partitions with Q/S tokens per node—the production strategy), the partition-to-node mapping is an explicit assignment table that must be stored and actively propagated. Topology cannot be derived mathematically from positions alone; it must be looked up in the table.

In both cases gossip is the distribution mechanism. What differs is the payload: under Strategy 1, each node gossips *"I exist at token position X."* Under Strategy 3, gossip carries the full partition assignment table. We will examine this distinction and its operational consequences in Section 4.3, after introducing the coordinator and the preference list.

3.2 The Naive Solution: The "Master" Registry

The natural engineering instinct is to create a central authority—a Configuration Server such as Apache ZooKeeper or a dedicated load balancer.

- **Process:** When a new node joins, it registers with the Master. When a node dies, the Master removes it. All other nodes poll the Master every few seconds to download the updated membership list.

3.2.1 Trouble with the Centralized Solution

This design has two fundamental problems:

- **Single Point of Failure (SPOF):** If the Master goes down, the entire cluster loses the ability to route traffic.
- **The Symmetry Principle:** Dynamo's design philosophy requires every node to be a peer—no node holds a privileged role. Introducing a Master creates a hierarchy, which creates both a bottleneck and a target for failure. This is the same force that drove us away from a single-primary database in Chapter 1: at sufficient scale, any single point of serialization becomes the weakest link in the system.

3.3 The Solution: Gossip Protocol

Instead of a central authority, Dynamo borrows from the peer-to-peer world. The **gossip protocol** has nodes share information periodically and perpetually with each other.

As an analogy, *instead of a Company All-Hands Meeting* (the CEO broadcasts to the whole staff), we rely on the *Office Breakroom* (employees share a rumor one-on-one, and it organically spreads to the entire building by lunch).

More formally, this family of algorithms is called *Epidemic Algorithms*. The goal is to spread information through the cluster the way a virus spreads through a population: exponentially fast, with no central broadcaster.

3.3.1 How it Works (The Heartbeat)

A note on fidelity to the original Dynamo design: the heartbeat-counter scheme described here is the standard way gossip-based membership is taught, and it is how Cassandra-style systems track liveness. Dynamo's own protocol is narrower. Its gossip reconciles each node's persisted membership-change history—the explicit join and leave events an administrator issues—and it detects failures locally through request non-response rather than through a heartbeat counter. Early designs of Dynamo did use a gossip-style failure detector, but the team later removed it (paper §4.8.3). We keep the heartbeat model here because it makes the convergence mechanics concrete; section 3.5 returns to what Dynamo actually does.

Every node maintains a **membership table**: a list of all nodes it knows about, along with a **heartbeat counter** and a timestamp recording when each entry was last updated. The counter is a simple logical integer—**not a wall-clock timestamp**—that each node increments every second to signal that it is alive. We do not use wall-clock time due to fundamental difficulties in synchronizing them across nodes. (The local timestamp with the counter is to know the recency of the last local update in the counter; those timestamps are not shared with peer nodes.) The mechanics are:

- **The Pulse:** Every second, Server A wakes up and increments its own heartbeat counter.
- **The Partner:** Server A picks one random peer from its membership table—say, Server B.
- **The Exchange:** Server A and Server B swap their complete membership tables:
  - Server A sends: `[A:105, B:99, C:40]`

  - Server B sends: `[A:100, B:102, C:40]`

  The entry `C:40` means both servers last heard Server C's heartbeat counter at 40. That number is a **logical counter**—not a timestamp—that Server C has incremented 40 times. It carries no relationship to wall-clock time.

- **The Merge:** Each node updates its table by keeping the highest counter value for every entry:
  - Server B sees that A's counter for itself is 105 vs. 100 in its own table. It updates its record for A.
  - Server A sees that B's counter for itself is 102 vs. 99 in its own table. It updates its record for B.

Over multiple rounds, fresh information propagates outward. Old entries are overwritten by higher counter values. No central coordinator is involved at any step. Communicating nodes can piggyback other information—such as token-to-node mappings—on the heartbeat message. If a node has not heard any heartbeat from node X for long enough, node X can be marked locally as unreachable, and that suspicion can piggyback to other peers in future heartbeat messages.

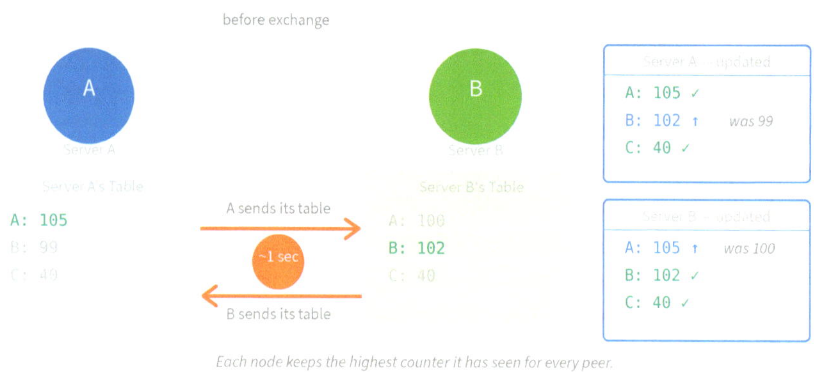

Figure 3.1 **The push-pull heartbeat exchange.** Every second, Server A selects a random peer (here, Server B) and both nodes swap their complete membership tables. Each node keeps the highest counter value for every entry. One exchange propagates A's freshest view of itself (105) to B, and B's freshest view of itself (102) to A. Because the exchange is bidirectional, gossip converges roughly twice as fast as a one-way push protocol.

3.3.2 The Power of Exponentials

Gossip sounds chaotic, but it is mathematically fast to converge. If Server A learns that Server Z just joined, it tells one neighbor. That neighbor tells one more, and so on:

- Round 1: 2 nodes know.
- Round 2: 4 nodes know.
- Round 3: 8 nodes know.

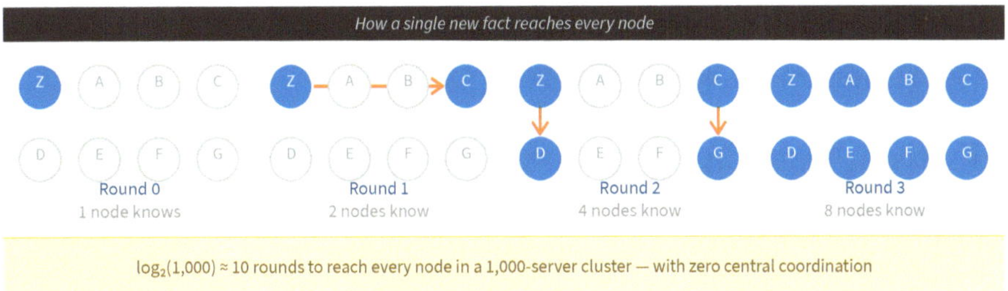

Figure 3.2 **Exponential convergence of gossip.** Each informed node picks one new random peer per round. The number of nodes that know a piece of information doubles every round, reaching every node in a 1,000-server cluster in roughly 10 rounds—a few seconds of wall-clock time—with zero central coordination.

In a cluster of 1,000 nodes, a state change reaches every node in roughly $\log_2(1{,}000) \approx 10$ rounds—a few seconds of wall-clock time, with zero central coordination.

One subtlety worth noting: Dynamo's gossip is **push-pull**, not just push. When Server A contacts Server B, both nodes exchange their full membership tables and update each other in the same interaction. This means the protocol converges roughly twice as fast as a pure push variant, and it is robust to dropped messages because the exchange repeats every second.

> **Aside: Thinking Exercise: Gossip Across Continents**
>
> In our discussion above, we assume that all nodes are co-located in the same data center, so propagation delay is negligible and gossip rounds complete in milliseconds. Consider: if the nodes of the ring were geographically distributed across multiple continents, would you still use a gossip protocol for cluster membership? Or would you use something else? What changes when propagation

> latency is measured in hundreds of milliseconds rather than microseconds?
> Hold this question in mind as you read Chapter 4. The tension between propagation delay and consistency guarantees will resurface when we discuss cross-region replication and the preference list.

3.4 The "Seed Node" Twist (Preventing Logical Partitions)

The gossip algorithm has one bootstrapping flaw.

Imagine starting a brand-new cluster of 50 nodes at the exact same millisecond. How will they know who else exists on the ring? Each node has an empty membership table. With no initial peer to gossip with, the cluster cannot self-assemble.

3.4.1 The Fix

Dynamo designates a small set of **Seed Nodes**—highly available, long-running servers whose addresses are hardcoded into the cluster configuration (or reachable via a well-known DNS name). Every node, in addition to its random gossip rounds, must eventually gossip with at least one seed node.

> **Aside: Seed Node Addressing in Production**
>
> Seed node addresses are typically expressed as DNS names rather than raw IP addresses—for example, `seed1.dynamo.internal`. The reason is that the seed address is hardcoded into every node's configuration (that is the whole point—a fixed, known rendezvous point). If a seed were hardcoded as a raw IP and that physical server were later replaced or moved, every node in the cluster would carry a stale address until its configuration was updated and redeployed. Pointing nodes at a DNS name instead means the IP can change behind the scenes—only the DNS record is updated, not the configuration of every node. Node software must still be robust to DNS resolution failures. Local caching of last-known seed addresses and exponential back-off on retry are standard mitigations. Several high-profile incidents at large cloud providers have been traced to cascading DNS resolution failures, making this a non-trivial operational concern.

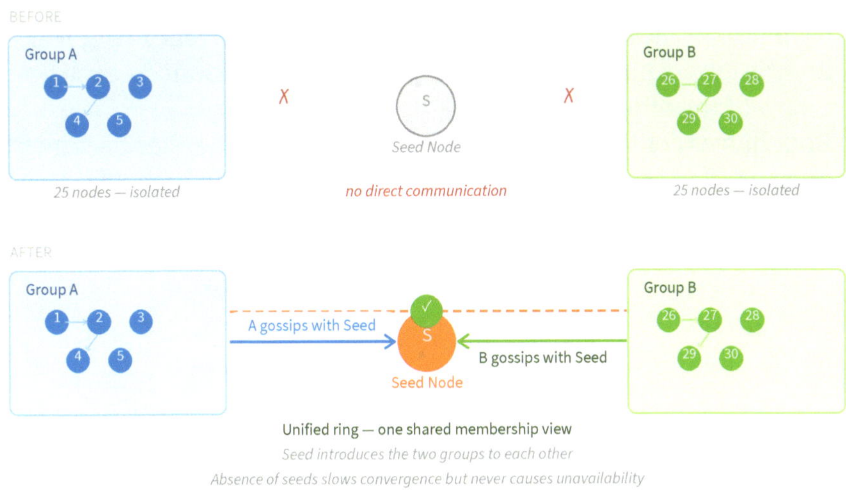

Figure 3.3 **How seed nodes prevent logical partitions.** Without seeds, a network failure during startup can leave two groups forming separate rings, each unaware of the other (top). Once both groups gossip with any seed node, the seed acts as a rendezvous bridge and the two membership views merge into one unified ring (bottom). The seed is a convergence accelerator, not a master: the system remains fully operational throughout, and the absence of seeds delays convergence but does not cause data loss or unavailability.

Seed nodes act as bridges. Suppose a network failure splits 50 new nodes into two groups that never gossip directly with each other. When the network partition heals, as soon as Group A contacts any seed and Group B contacts any seed, the seed introduces the two groups to each other and the two independent membership views merge into one.

An important clarification: seed nodes are not the centralized Master we rejected in section 3.2. The Dynamo design notes that the absence of seed connectivity *slows* convergence but does not cause correctness or availability failures—the system remains operational once nodes discover each other through any path. Seeds are a convergence accelerator, not a control plane authority.

> ### Aside: Ring Fragmentation
>
> Suppose we commission 50 new nodes simultaneously. At that exact moment, a network switch failure partitions them such that: Nodes 1–25 can gossip only with each other. They form a self-consistent membership ring. Nodes 26–50 can gossip only with

> each other. They form a second, separate ring. This is a **ring fragmentation** scenario: two independent Dynamo instances, each unaware of the other's existence.
> Both halves continue to accept reads and writes—neither becomes unavailable. The implications for data consistency are addressed in Chapters 5 and 7. When the network heals, the gossip protocol converges on a unified membership table. Seed nodes, if reachable, accelerate this healing by acting as rendezvous points for both groups.

3.5 Failure Detection: "You Look Quiet..."

Gossip serves a second purpose beyond membership: it is the mechanism through which the cluster detects that a node has failed. Dead servers cannot send "I am dead" messages. Instead, as described in the Dynamo paper (§4.8.3), Dynamo uses a **purely local notion of failure detection** based on message non-response.

When Server A sends any message to Server B—a gossip exchange, a get or put request, or any other inter-node call—and B fails to respond, Server A immediately marks B as unavailable for its own routing decisions. No cluster-wide vote is required. Because gossip exchanges happen every second, unresponsiveness surfaces quickly even on a cluster with low client traffic. Server A then routes around B using alternate nodes and periodically retries B to check for recovery.

The failure observation then propagates through the cluster via gossip:

- Server A observes that B has not responded to its messages and marks B as **Suspect** locally.
- Server A gossips this to Server C: "I haven't heard from B recently."
- If Server C has also found B unresponsive, the suspicion reaches consensus. The cluster collectively stops routing requests to B.

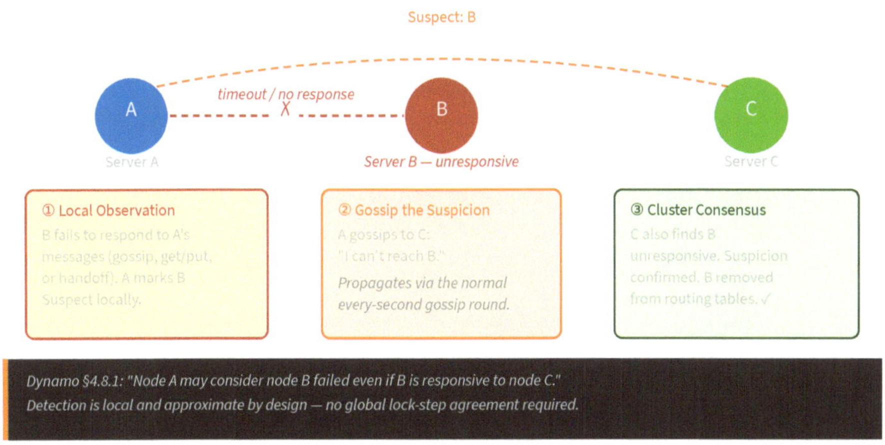

Figure 3.4 **Dynamo's three-step implicit failure detection.** A node is declared suspect when it fails to respond to another node's request (①). The observing node gossips this suspicion to its peers (②). When multiple nodes independently observe it unresponsive, the cluster reaches consensus and removes the node from routing (③). Per the Dynamo design, detection is intentionally local and approximate: Server A may route around Server B even if B is reachable from Server C. This avoids the cost of a global agreement protocol just to mark a node as unavailable.

Crucially, Dynamo's failure detection is intentionally approximate and local. The paper explicitly states that it is acceptable for Server A to consider Server B failed even if B is responsive to Server C. This avoids the cost of a global agreement protocol just to mark a node as unavailable. The cluster favors availability of routing decisions over perfect accuracy of failure state.

> ### Aside: Byzantine Faults and Asymmetric Partitions
>
> The gossip protocol assumes that nodes are non-malicious and that messages in transit cannot be tampered with. In practice, this is enforced by mutual TLS or similar transport-layer security. If nodes could act arbitrarily or maliciously, the cluster would require Byzantine Fault Tolerant (BFT) protocols instead. Dynamo operates under the assumption that all nodes belong to a single administrative entity running vetted software, so the simpler crash-fault-tolerant model is sufficient.
>
> A subtler issue: network failures can create **asymmetric reachability**. If Server A cannot reach Server B, but Server C can reach Server B just fine, then A and C hold different views of B's liveness.

> This is called an **asymmetric partition**. Dynamo handles this correctly because failure detection is local: Server A routes around B for its own requests, while C continues to use B normally. The inconsistency resolves naturally once A can communicate with B again—no global lock-step agreement is required. This is precisely the availability-preserving trade-off that Dynamo was designed to make.

3.6 What Gossip Is—and Is Not—For

This distinction is fundamental and frequently missed. Dynamo gossips strictly over the **control plane**. It never gossips data (keys and values).

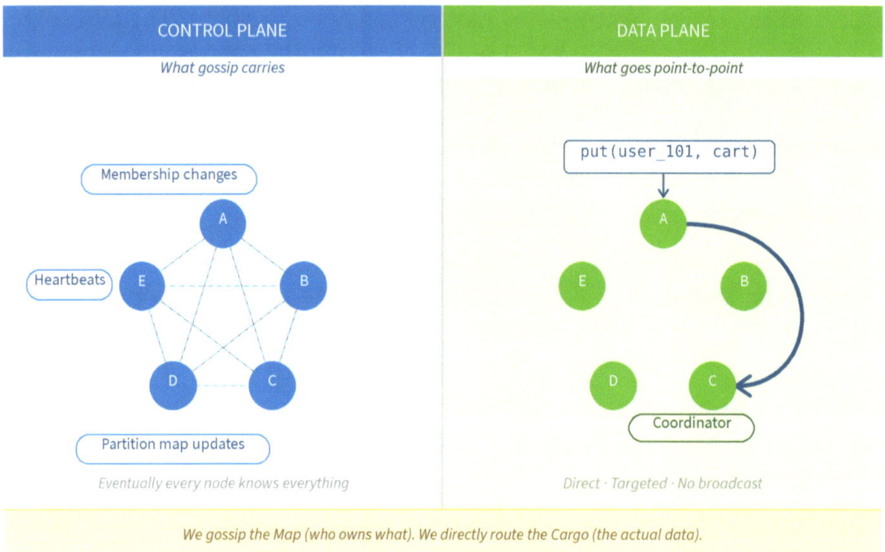

Figure 3.5 **The control plane versus the data plane.** Gossip propagates cluster metadata—membership, heartbeat counters, partition maps—to all nodes via epidemic broadcast, so every node eventually holds a complete routing table (left). Actual read and write requests travel directly and exclusively via point-to-point routing to the specific coordinator responsible for that key (right). Using gossip for data would make the system orders of magnitude slower and would saturate the network with unnecessary traffic.

Where Dynamo *does* use gossip (the control plane):

A background process on each node randomly selects a peer every second and exchanges membership state:

- **Membership and ring state:** When a new node joins or an administrator changes partition assignments, this information is gossiped. Eventually every node knows exactly who is in the cluster and which partitions they own.

- **Failure detection:** Nodes share heartbeat counters and local suspicion information via gossip. The cluster reaches eventual consensus about which nodes are alive.
- **Routing table synchronization:** Because every node receives gossiped membership updates, every node maintains a complete, locally cached copy of the routing table. Any node can forward a request directly to the correct coordinator—no centralized load balancer required.

Where Dynamo does *not* use gossip (the data plane):

- **Read and write requests:** A write for a shopping cart is sent point-to-point directly to the coordinator responsible for that key. It is not broadcast to the ring.
- **Replication:** The coordinator sends data directly to the N specific replica nodes on the preference list, relying on a reliable point-to-point transport (e.g., TCP) to guarantee delivery—rather than gossip's probabilistic, eventual-delivery broadcast.
- **Anti-entropy:** Merkle tree synchronization (covered in Chapter 6) is a targeted, one-to-one conversation between two specific replica nodes that share the same key range. It is not a cluster-wide broadcast.

We gossip the Map (who owns what). We directly route the Cargo (the actual read/write data).

3.7 Summary

We now have a system that is:

- **Decentralized:** No master node to crash. Every node is a peer.
- **Scalable:** Adding nodes adds more gossip partners, not more load on a central server. Convergence time grows as $O(\log N)$ where N is the number of nodes in the ring.
- **Self-aware:** Permanent membership changes—a node being decommissioned or a new node being added—are explicit: an administrator issues the join or leave command, and gossip propagates that change to the rest of the cluster. Gossip's own detection machinery is aimed at the messier case it cannot get an explicit signal for: a node that goes silent without anyone telling the cluster it left, whether from a crash,

a network blip, or an overload. In both cases, the cluster converges on a consistent view without any central coordinator.

One important property to internalize before moving on: gossip guarantees **eventual** convergence, not instantaneous consistency of cluster state. For a brief window after any membership change, different nodes may hold slightly different views of the ring. This is expected and acceptable. The system does not require every node to have an identical, up-to-the-millisecond membership table. Quorums, covered in Chapter 5, are designed to work correctly even when nodes have mildly divergent views of the cluster.

Now that nodes can find each other, we can start storing data. But storing data on a single node—even the correct owner on the ring—creates a catastrophic vulnerability: if that node's disk dies, the data is gone. We need insurance. We need replication.

References

- *DeCandia, G., et al., "Dynamo: Amazon's Highly Available Key-Value Store," ACM SOSP, 2007. §4.8 (Membership and Failure Detection), §4.8.1 (Ring Membership), §4.8.2 (External Discovery).*
- *Demers, A., Greene, D., Hauser, C., Irish, W., Larson, J., Shenker, S., Sturgis, H., Swinehart, D., and Terry, D., "Epidemic Algorithms for Replicated Database Maintenance," ACM PODC, 1987.*
- *Hayashibara, N., Defago, X., Yared, R., and Katayama, T., "The ϕ Accrual Failure Detector," IEEE SRDS, 2004.*

CHAPTER 4

Insurance Against Loss (Replication)

In traditional databases, you often rely on RAID (Redundant Array of Independent Disks) to guard against disk failure. In distributed systems, however, we must plan for failures at a much larger scale. An entire datacenter building might lose power, or a network partition might cut off a whole region. A RAID controller cannot save you if the server itself is physically destroyed.

To guarantee that a shopping cart survives a catastrophe, we cannot store it in one place. We must **replicate** it across multiple, physically independent machines.

4.1 The Replication Factor N

The Dynamo system introduces a simple configuration variable: **N**, the ***Replication Factor***—the total number of unique physical nodes that must hold a copy of each data item. The Dynamo system describes N as a parameter configured *"per-instance"*, so different Dynamo deployments can choose different values based on their durability and cost requirements.

Why make this tunable rather than hard-coding a value? Different workloads need different guarantees. Financial transaction records may warrant N = 5, while a transient session cache might be fine with N = 2. By increasing N, we obtain more replicas; if those replicas fail independently, overall durability increases exponentially—though at the cost of additional storage and write coordination overhead.

Standard setting used in the Dynamo system: N = 3. With three replicas on separate machines, the data survives even if one server crashes and a second is simultaneously taken offline for maintenance.

> Aside: The Mathematics of Replication

In distributed systems, we do not *guess* about reliability—we **engineer** it. Whether we are calculating Availability (uptime) or Durability (data survival), the fundamental mathematics rest on the probability of independent failures. The core rule: *to find the probability that multiple independent events all occur simultaneously, multiply their individual probabilities.*

Part 1 — The Forward Calculation: Measuring the Gain. Assume we are using commodity hard drives. A single drive has a realistic annual failure rate of 5%:

Probability of failure for a single node: $p = 0.05$

Probability of survival for a single node: $1 - p = 0.95$ (95% durable)

In a distributed system, data is permanently lost only if **all** replicas fail simultaneously before the system can heal. If we create N replicas, the probability of complete data loss is the probability that Replica 1 fails *and* Replica 2 fails, all the way through Replica N. The formula for the system's Durability D is:

$$D = 1 - p^N$$

Let's watch how quickly durability increases as we add replicas:

- **N = 1:** $D = 1 - 0.05^1 = 0.95 \rightarrow$ 95.0% durability
- **N = 2:** $D = 1 - 0.05^2 = 1 - 0.0025 = 0.9975 \rightarrow$ 99.75% durability
- **N = 3:** $D = 1 - 0.05^3 = 1 - 0.000125 = 0.999875 \rightarrow$ ~99.99% durability

By moving from one disk to three, we went from a system that loses 1 file in 20, to one that loses 1 file in nearly 10,000. This **exponential decrease** in failure probability is the core principle behind distributed storage.

Replicas (N)	Failure Prob.	Durability D	1 Loss per how many files
N = 1	p	95.00%	1 in 20
N = 2	p^2	99.75%	1 in 400
N = 3	p^3	99.99%	1 in 8,000
N = 4	p^4	99.9994%	1 in 160,000

Part 2 — The Reverse Calculation: Engineering for a Target. In the real world, engineers usually work *backward*. The business does not ask "What is our durability if we buy 4 servers?"—it says "We need Six Nines of durability (99.9999%). How many servers do we need to buy?" We can reverse our formula to solve for N. Start with the durability target:

$$1 - p^N \geq \text{Target}$$

Isolate the failure probability:

$$p^N \leq 1 - \text{Target}$$

Apply logarithms to bring the exponent down. Note: because $\log p$ is negative for $0 < p < 1$, dividing by it **flips the inequality sign:**

$$N \cdot \log p \leq \log(1 - \text{Target})$$

$$N \geq \frac{\log(1 - \text{Target})}{\log p}$$

A Practical Example: Your company mandates 99.9999% durability (Target = 0.999999) on cloud instances with an individual failure rate of 2% ($p = 0.02$). Plug in:

- $N \geq \log(1 - 0.999999)/\log(0.02)$
- $N \geq \log(0.000001)/\log(0.02)$
- $N \geq (-6)/(-1.698)$
- $N \geq 3.53$

Since we cannot build a fraction of a server, we always take the ceiling. Therefore, to hit Six Nines of durability with a 2% per-node failure rate, we must set our replication factor to **N = 4.**

A Crucial Engineering Caveat — The Independence Assumption. This beautiful mathematics rests entirely on one massive assumption: **independent failures**. If $p = 0.05$ represents a hard drive failing on its own, the math holds. But if you place all three replicas in the same physical server rack, and the rack's power supply blows out, the failures are no longer independent. The probability of all three going down is no longer 0.05^3—it collapses back to just 0.05. This is why real storage systems are designed to place replicas not just on different nodes, but in **different data centers entirely**. Mathematical redundancy only works when physical isolation actually guarantees it. As a practical note: if physical distance between data centers becomes large, propagation delay also increases, so placing replicas in a nearby (within a few miles) data center can balance durability against write latency.

4.2 The Coordinator: The Quarterback

When a write request (say, “Add iPad to Cart”) arrives at the cluster, a load balancer routes it to some node in the ring. That node checks whether it falls within the **top N nodes of the preference list** (the ordered list of physically distinct nodes responsible for a given key—constructed in section 4.3) for the requested key. If it does, it becomes the **Coordinator** and handles the write directly. If not, it forwards the request to the first node among the top N nodes in the preference list.

The Coordinator’s job is not merely to save the data locally. Upon receiving a `put()` request, the Coordinator:

- **Generates a version vector** for the new version of the data.
- **Writes the new version locally**.
- **Sends the new version** to the (N-1) highest-ranked reachable nodes in the preference list.
- Waits for at least **W-1** of those nodes to respond before declaring the write successful (where W is the write quorum introduced in Chapter 5).

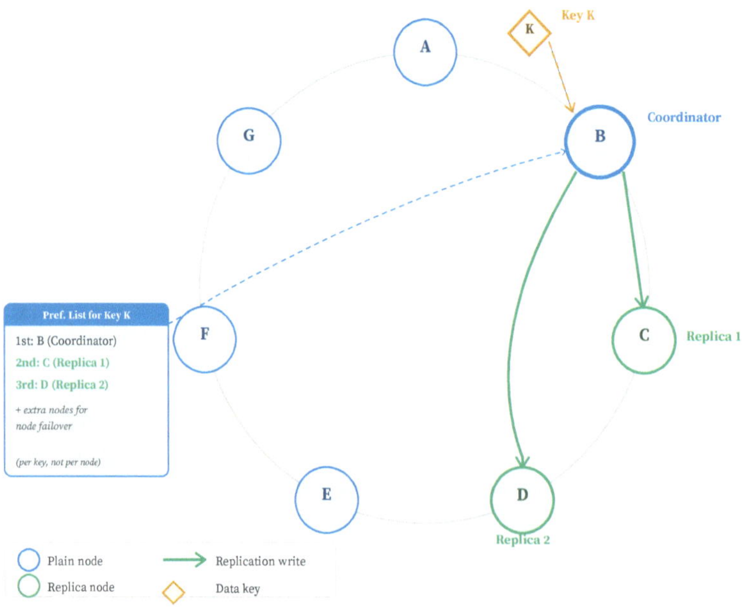

Figure 4.1 **Coordinator B stores Key K locally and replicates it to nodes C and D**—the next two distinct physical nodes clockwise on the ring (N = 3).

Importantly, the Coordinator role is not fixed to a single machine. *Any* of the top N nodes in the preference list can act as Coordinator. In practice, Dynamo chooses the node that replied fastest to the previous read for the same key—an optimization that increases the likelihood of achieving *"read-your-writes"* consistency and reduces tail latency at the 99.9th percentile.

4.3 The Preference List: More than the Next Neighbor

The **preference list** is the ordered set of nodes responsible for storing a particular key. Its construction contains two important subtleties that are easy to overlook.

4.3.1 The Virtual-Node Trap

Recall from Chapter 2 that one physical server operates as many **virtual nodes** (tokens) scattered across the ring—potentially hundreds of positions. The naïve assumption—"just pick the next N positions clockwise"—creates a dangerous trap.

Imagine walking clockwise from Key K's position and encountering:

- Position 1: Virtual Node A1 (owned by Server A)
- Position 2: Virtual Node A2 (owned by Server A)
- Position 3: Virtual Node A3 (owned by Server A)

Three logical nodes, but all on **the same physical machine**. If Server A fails, you lose all three replicas simultaneously. Your replication factor of N = 3 was an illusion—it was actually N = 1.

4.3.2 The Solution: Physical Diversity

The preference list is constructed by walking the ring clockwise and **skipping positions that belong to physical nodes already in the list**, until N *distinct physical nodes* have been selected.

Furthermore, the preference list deliberately contains **more than N nodes** to account for node failures. If one of the top N nodes is unreachable, the system can fall back to the next eligible node on the list without violating physical diversity.

In advanced deployments, the preference list construction can also enforce **rack awareness**—ensuring that replicas are placed on distinct physical racks or in different data center Availability Zones, so that a single power-distribution failure cannot destroy multiple replicas simultaneously.

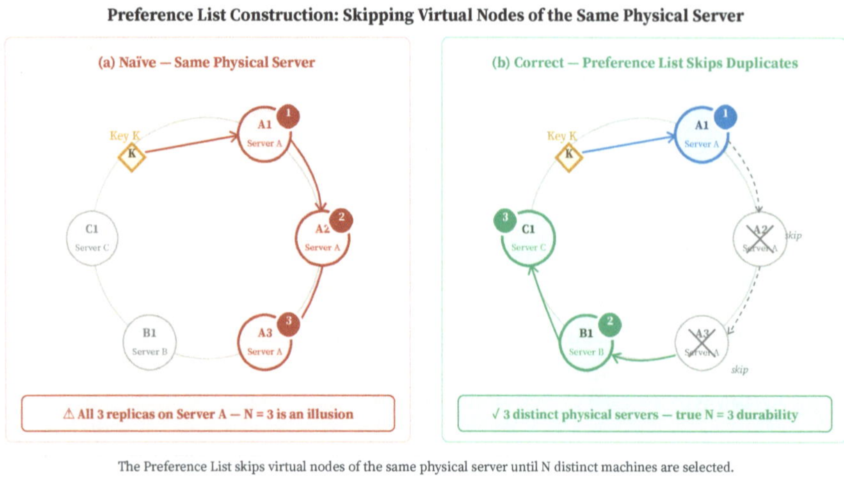

Figure 4.2 **(a) The naïve approach picks three virtual nodes of the same physical server**—catastrophic if that server fails. **(b) The correct preference list** skips Server A's duplicate virtual nodes and selects one slot from each of A, B, and C.

Aside: Rack Awareness and the Illusion of Independence

In the *Mathematics of Replication* sidebar, we proved that adding replicas exponentially increases durability—but only if failures are **statistically independent.** That assumption is more fragile than it looks. If three servers are bolted into the same metal rack, they share the same **Top-of-Rack (ToR) network switch** and the same physical **Power Distribution Unit (PDU).** If someone trips over that rack's power cable, or the PDU's circuit breaker trips, all three servers go dark instantly. Your carefully engineered p^3 just collapsed back to $p = 0.05$. The math is still correct—but the physical independence it assumed never existed.

To prevent this, distributed systems must possess **Rack Awareness**: knowledge of the physical layout of the server floor so they can deliberately scatter replicas across different *fault domains*—groups of hardware that share a common failure point. But how does a piece of software know where it lives in the physical world?

1. The On-Premises Approach: IP Inferring. In a traditional data center, network administrators design the IP schema to map exactly to the physical floor plan. Every ToR switch is assigned a dedicated subnet. For example, a system might be configured so that the **3rd octet of an IP address represents the rack number:**

- Node A: `10.42.`**`15`**`.22` (Rack 15)

- Node B: `10.42.`**`15`**`.89` (Rack 15)
- Node C: `10.42.`**`16`**`.10` (Rack 16)

When the database coordinator is deciding where to place Replica 2, it runs a simple script—often called a **"Snitch"** in systems like Cassandra—to inspect the IP addresses of candidate nodes. It sees that Node A and Node B share the .15 subnet, concludes they are on the same rack, and intentionally skips Node B. It places the replica on Node C in Rack 16 instead, ensuring physical isolation.

2. The Cloud Approach: Abstracted Fault Domains. In modern cloud environments (AWS, Azure, GCP), the underlying physical racks are hidden behind heavy network virtualization. You cannot rely on IP addresses to deduce physical location—the cloud provider assigns them arbitrarily. Instead, cloud providers expose explicit APIs for fault isolation:

Micro-Isolation — Spread Placement Groups: By launching virtual machines into a "Spread Placement Group," the cloud provider's control plane *mathematically guarantees* that each instance is placed on a distinct physical hardware rack with its own independent network and power source. This is the cloud equivalent of the on-premises Snitch.

Macro-Isolation — Availability Zones (AZs): By placing replicas in different Availability Zones (e.g., us-east-1a and us-east-1b), replicas land in entirely separate data center buildings, often miles apart, with independent power grids, cooling systems, and network ingress. This protects against massive correlated failures: floods, regional power outages, fires, or even a backhoe cutting a fiber trunk.

How Dynamo Applies This: When a node in Dynamo routes a write request, it does not simply pick the next N positions on the consistent hashing ring. It builds a **Preference List**—walking clockwise around the ring and skipping any node that shares the same physical rack or data center as a node already selected, until it has found N physically isolated targets.

Aside: How Each Node Knows the Ring—Strategy 1 vs. Strategy 3

For the Coordinator to know *which* nodes belong to the preference list of a given key, every node must maintain a map of the ring. The two strategies differ fundamentally in how that map is built and stored.

Strategy 1 — Topology by Math (Implicit). Each node gossips its tokens (random hash positions). Any recipient can sort the full token list and derive the ring topology by arithmetic: "My token is 50; the next in sorted order is 90; therefore the node at 90 is my successor." The ring self-assembles in every node's memory with no central authority and no administrator. The gossip payload is minimal: *"I exist at token X."* Receivers recompute the ring topology locally from the updated token list. But the membership table each node must store grows as **S** × **T** (S = number of physical nodes in the cluster, T = tokens per node)—all tokens from all nodes. Each token is a raw 128-bit MD5 hash with no structure, so nothing can be compressed away. With S=30 nodes each holding T tokens, every node stores 30T entries. For Strategy 1 to achieve good load balance, T must be large—because load imbalance decreases only as $1/\sqrt{S \times T}$, the probabilistic convergence of random placement. Driving imbalance below 5% requires T ≈ 300–500, pushing the table to 9,000–15,000 entries per node and still climbing.

Strategy 3 — Topology by Partition Table (Explicit). With equal-sized fixed partitions there is no mathematical relationship between a node's identity and its partition assignments. Every node must store an explicit **Partition** → **Owner** mapping table of Q entries—one per partition—and gossip the current table to peers so the full ring state propagates. The gossip payload is larger per message: *"Here is the current partition map."* But—and this is the key—Strategy 3 achieves near-perfect load balance **by construction**, not by probability. Because partitions are equal-sized by definition, you do not need a large Q to approximate uniformity. Q = 120 (four partitions per node with S=30) already yields ≥97% efficiency. The problem is *designed away*, not *converged away*. Each entry in the table is a compact (partition ID, node ID) pair—sequential integers, not random hashes—so the table at Q=120 is tiny compared to Strategy 1's token list at T=300.

The Metadata Gap. The chart below approximates Figure 8 of the original Dynamo paper. The x-axis is log-scaled to make the gap visible. Strategy 3 (teal, solid) reaches near-optimal efficiency at fewer than ∼1,000 metadata units. Strategy 1 (blue, dashed) needs ∼35,000 units to reach comparable efficiency—and never fully gets there, because random placement cannot guarantee uniformity the way fixed partitions can.

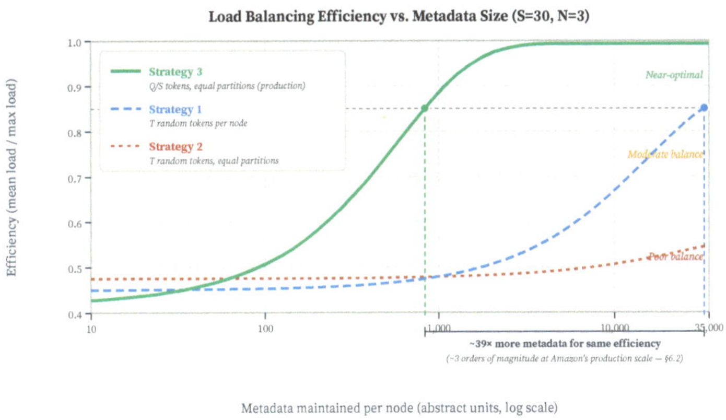

Figure 4.3 **Load Balancing Efficiency vs. Metadata Size — Strategy 1 vs. Strategy 3 (S = 30, N = 3).** Strategy 3 reaches near-optimal efficiency (∼97%) at fewer than 1,000 metadata units; Strategy 1 requires ∼35,000 units for comparable efficiency—a gap of ∼40× at this scale, growing to ∼3 orders of magnitude in Amazon's production deployment (paper §6.2). Strategy 2 (red, dotted) underperforms even Strategy 1: it still assigns whole fixed partitions winner-take-all by the same random tokens, so more tokens do not smooth out the imbalance the way Strategy 1's directly-summed ranges do. X-axis is log-scaled. Approximates Figure 8, DeCandia et al., SOSP 2007.

Original Dynamo system reported that Strategy 3 "reduces the size of membership information maintained at each node by three orders of magnitude" compared to Strategy 1. Our chart shows ∼40× at the modelled S=30 scale; the full 1,000× emerges at Amazon's production node counts where S is in the hundreds and T needed for acceptable balance in Strategy 1 grows proportionally. The gap is structural, not incidental: Strategy 1 needs large T because it is fighting the Birthday Paradox with probability; Strategy 3 makes the Birthday Paradox irrelevant by fixing the geometry.

Why the smaller table matters for gossip. Membership information is gossiped periodically between every pair of nodes. A smaller payload means lower bandwidth consumption, faster convergence, and lower CPU overhead for deserialization. At hundreds of nodes gossiping every second, a 1,000× payload reduction is the difference between gossip being invisible background noise and being a measurable fraction of cluster traffic.

Beyond metadata size, Strategy 3 also enables **faster bootstrapping** (fixed partition files can be transferred whole rather than

> scanned key-by-key) and **simpler archival** (enumerate Q partition files rather than scatter-gather across all nodes). These operational benefits, combined with the metadata reduction, are why Amazon migrated from Strategy 1 to Strategy 3 in production.

4.4 Synchronous vs. Asynchronous Replication

The Coordinator now knows *who* the N replicas are. The next question is: **do we wait for them before responding to the client?**

4.4.1 Option A — Synchronous (Wait for All)

The Coordinator sends data to all N nodes and waits for every one of them to confirm "Saved!" before reporting success to the client.

- **Pro:** Maximum safety—data is confirmed durable on all N machines before the client proceeds.
- **Con:** The response latency equals the slowest replica. One sluggish or temporarily overloaded node stalls every write.

4.4.2 Option B — Asynchronous (Return Early)

The Coordinator writes locally, immediately tells the client "Success," and propagates copies to the other N-1 nodes in the background.

- **Pro:** Near-instant response for the client.
- **Con:** If the Coordinator crashes before the background replication completes, the data is lost with no record that the write ever occurred.

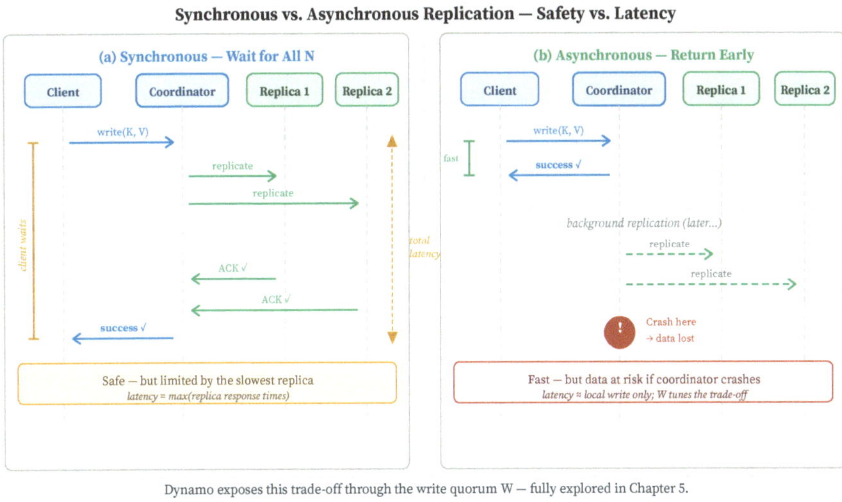

Figure 4.4 **(a) Synchronous replication:** the client waits until all N nodes acknowledge, maximizing safety at the cost of latency. **(b) Asynchronous replication:** the client receives success immediately while remaining replicas are updated in the background.

Neither extreme is universally correct. Dynamo avoids hard-coding either option. Instead, it exposes this trade-off through the configurable **write quorum parameter W**—the minimum number of nodes that must acknowledge a write before success is returned. Setting W = N is fully synchronous; W = 1 is maximally asynchronous. The full algebra of N, R, and W is the subject of the next chapter.

4.5 Summary

This chapter established the **where** of durability: which N physically distinct machines should hold each copy of the data, and why physical diversity is not optional. The key takeaways grounded in the Dynamo system are:

- **N is a per-instance parameter**—typically N = 3—balancing durability, cost, and performance.
- **The preference list** contains *more than* N nodes to accommodate failures and skips virtual nodes of the same physical server to guarantee true physical diversity.
- **The Coordinator** is whichever node among the top N is chosen to handle a given request; it forwards writes to the N highest-ranked reachable nodes in the preference list.

- **Rack and datacenter awareness** is essential: replication without physical isolation is a mathematical fiction.
- **The synchronous/asynchronous spectrum** will be formalized in Chapter 5 as the quorum parameters R and W, giving application developers a precise knob to tune the safety–latency trade-off.

We have defined *where* the data lives. The next chapter asks: **how many of those N copies must confirm an operation before we consider it done?** That is the question of quorums—and the answer is one of the most famous equations in distributed systems.

References

- *DeCandia, G., et al., "Dynamo: Amazon's Highly Available Key-Value Store," ACM SOSP, 2007. §4.3 (Replication), §4.5 (Execution of get() and put() Operations).*

CHAPTER 5

The Democracy of Data (Quorums)

In Chapter 4, we decided to store our shopping cart on three different servers (N = 3). Now imagine a user wants to read that cart.

- Do we ask Server A?
- Do we ask Server B?
- What if Server A thinks the cart has two items, but Server B thinks it has three? (Chapter 7ś shopping-cart walkthrough shows exactly how a network partition produces this kind of split-brain disagreement, and how version vectors let the system detect and reconcile it.)

In a distributed system, if we do not take special care, there may be no single "truth." The data can differ from replica to replica. To establish truth, we need a voting system. We need a **quorum**.

5.1 The Analogy: The Family Vote

Imagine a family of three people (N = 3) trying to decide where to go for dinner.

- **Unanimous (strict):** you go only if all three agree.
- *Problem:* if Dad is asleep, the family starves. The system is "unavailable."
- **Majority (quorum):** you go if two out of three agree.
- *Benefit:* you can still eat even if one person is missing.
- **Dictator (available):** if one person wants pizza, you get pizza.
- *Problem:* Mom might order sushi at the very same moment. Now you have a conflict—an inconsistency.

We can apply exactly this logic to the reads and writes of our key-value store.

5.2 The Magic Formula: N, R, and W

To tune the system, we expose three variables:

- **N (replication factor):** the total number of nodes that should hold the data (standard: 3).
- **R (read quorum):** the number of nodes we must hear from to consider a read successful.
- **W (write quorum):** the number of nodes that must confirm a write for it to be considered successful.

A small but important mechanical detail: the coordinator is itself one of the N nodes, and it writes the new version *locally* before forwarding it. A write is therefore declared successful once at least **W – 1** of the other replicas acknowledge it—the coordinator's own local write supplies the remaining vote. We will keep speaking loosely of "W nodes confirming," but remember that the coordinator is always one of them.

The relationship between these three numbers determines how the system behaves. The golden rule of quorum consistency is:

If R + W > N, the read set and the write set are guaranteed to overlap.

At least one node in any "read group" must also have been part of the most recent "write group." That single shared node is what lets a read observe the latest acknowledged write (Figure 5.1).

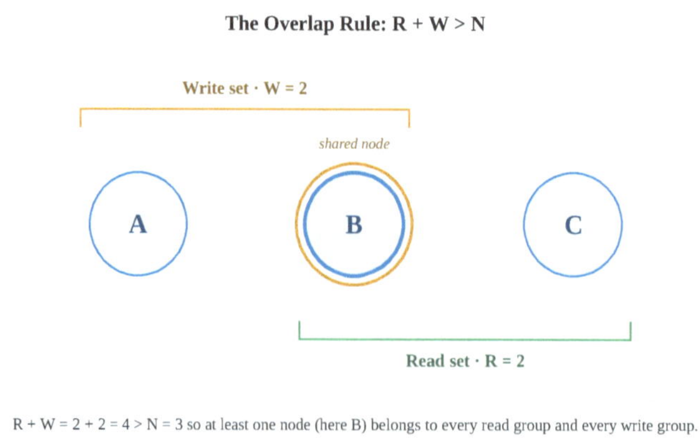

Figure 5.1 **The Overlap Rule.** A write of W = 2 and a read of R = 2 over N = 3 replicas must share at least one node. Because R + W = 4 exceeds N = 3, every read intersects the most recent acknowledged write—here, node B.

A note on what "overlap" buys you. The intersection guarantees that a read *touches* a node carrying the latest acknowledged write; it is not, by itself, the strong (linearizable) consistency of a single-master database. Concurrent writes can still produce divergent versions that a read will surface, and—as we are about to see—the guarantee weakens further once we relax the quorum into a "sloppy" one. R + W > N is a powerful overlap rule, not a promise that the system behaves like a single, perfectly serialized machine.

Aside: Quorum Overlap Is Not Linearizability

The R + W > N rule from Figure 5.1 guarantees that a read quorum intersects the write set of any write that has already *completed*. It is tempting to read this as "strong consistency," but it is not: it imposes no single global order on operations, and it says nothing about writes still in flight.

Take Figure 5.1's exact setup—N = 3 replicas A, B, C, with W = 2 and R = 2—and suppose all three start holding value v0 (meaning key v has value 0). Consider this history (Figure 5.2):

- A client issues **write(v1)**. The update reaches A first; A stores v1 and acknowledges. B and C have not yet received it, so the write has only 1 of its 2 required acks—it is *still in flight*, not yet successful.
- Client Y reads with the quorum {A, B}. A returns v1, B returns v0; because v1 descends from v0, the read returns **v1**. Y now believes the value is v1.
- After Y's read completes, client Z reads with the quorum {B, C}. Both still hold v0, so Z returns **v0**.

A later read (Z) returned an *older* value than an earlier read (Y)—yet both reads honored R + W > N. Linearizability forbids exactly this: once any client observes v1, no subsequent read may regress to v0. The overlap rule did not prevent it, because it only binds a read to the write set of a *completed* write; the v1 write had not yet reached its W replicas, so the guarantee simply did not cover it.

Quorums ensure you cannot *miss* a finished write—they do not order operations globally, nor stop two reads from disagreeing about an unfinished one. This is why linearizable quorum registers—the ABD construction, a classic algorithm (Attiya, Bar-Noy, and Dolev, 1995) for building a strongly consistent read/write register out of ordinary majority quorums—add a read **write-back**: before returning v1, the reader first propagates it to a full quorum, so a later read cannot fall back to v0. Dynamo's read-repair (discussed next) is best-effort cleanup, not such a barrier—one more reason this setup, (N, R, W) = (3, 2, 2), is *consistency-leaning*, not strongly consistent.

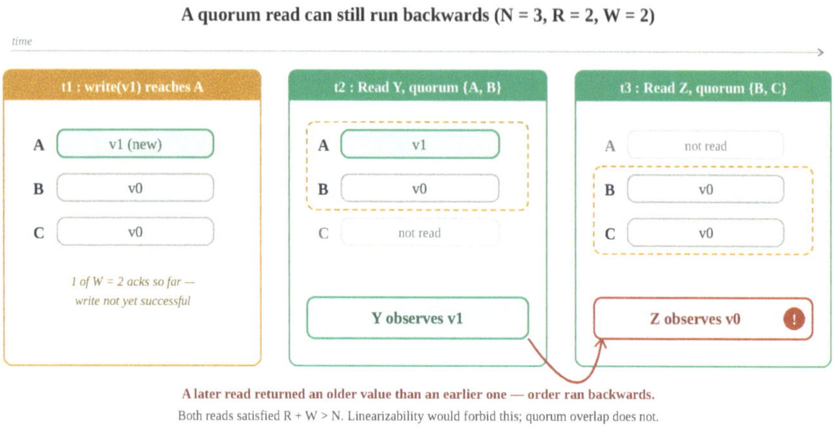

Figure 5.2 **Overlap is not linearizability.** A write of v1 that has reached only one of its W = 2 replicas is read by Y (quorum {A, B}) as v1, then by a later Z (quorum {B, C}) as v0. Both reads honor R + W > N, yet the observed value moves backwards—which linearizability forbids.

Aside: What Is Read Repair?

Every quorum read is also a chance to fix a stale replica. When the coordinator collects R responses for a `get()`, it sometimes finds that they do not all agree—one or more replicas answered with an older version. **Read repair** is what happens next: the coordinator still answers the client immediately with the newest version it found, and—in the background, without making the client wait—pushes that same version out to whichever replicas in *this read's* quorum were behind (Figure 5.3).

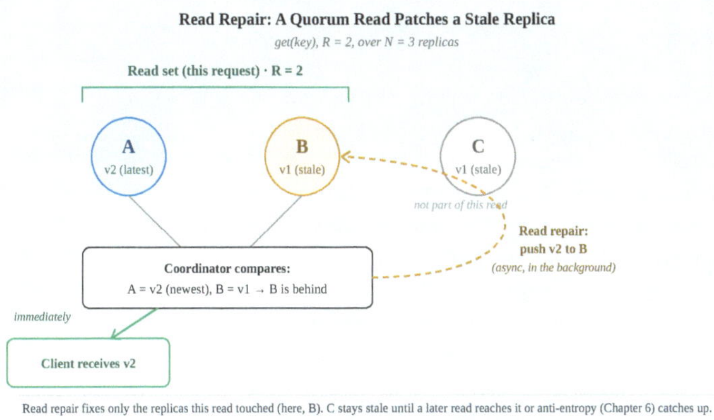

Figure 5.3 **Read Repair.** A get(key) with R = 2 touches A (v2, latest) and B (v1, stale). The coordinator answers the client immediately with v2, and separately pushes v2 to B in the background. C, untouched by this read, stays stale until a later read reaches it or anti-entropy catches up.
This is different from the synchronous write-back used by linearizable registers like ABD (discussed above): read repair is asynchronous and best-effort, not a barrier the client waits behind, and it only touches the replicas that happened to be part of this particular read. A replica that nobody happens to read stays stale until something else notices it—which is exactly the gap Chapter 6's anti-entropy process (Merkle trees) exists to close in the background, for keys nobody reads often enough to repair this way.
In production, read repair quietly does most of the work: popular keys get read constantly, so divergence is usually patched within the next handful of requests, long before anti-entropy ever needs to scan a Merkle tree for that key.

5.3 Tuning the Knobs (N, R, W)

We do not want a one-size-fits-all database. Clients of our store should be able to choose these numbers to match the job at hand (Figure 5.4).

5.3.1 Configuration A: the balanced default—(N, R, W) = (3, 2, 2)

- **Math:** $2 + 2 = 4 > 3$. Overlap holds.
- **Behavior:** a write waits for two nodes; a read consults two nodes. Because the sets overlap, a read sees the latest acknowledged write.
- **Cost:** the cluster tolerates exactly one unavailable node. If two of the three are down, both reads and writes stall.

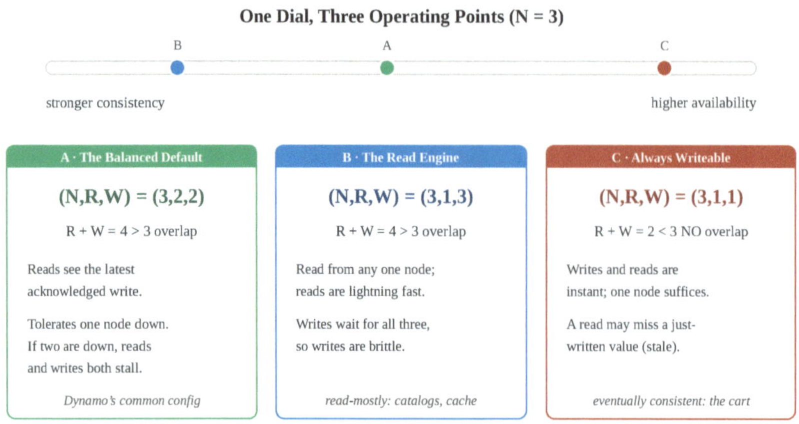

Figure 5.4 **One Dial, Three Operating Points.** The same N = 3 cluster can be tuned toward consistency or toward availability by moving R and W. Configurations A and B satisfy R + W > N (overlap); configuration C trades that overlap for raw availability.

This is the configuration the Dynamo system uses as the common production setting—the values most instances actually ran with to meet their performance, durability, consistency, and availability targets.

5.3.2 Configuration B: the high-performance read engine—(N, R, W) = (3, 1, 3)

- **Math:** 3 + 1 = 4 > 3. Overlap holds.
- **Behavior:** writes are slow (every replica must acknowledge), but reads are lightning fast—any single available node can answer.
- **Use case:** data that is read constantly and written rarely—product catalogs, promotional listings, or an authoritative persistence cache. The Dynamo system describes exactly this "high-performance read engine" profile, with R set to 1 and W set to N.

5.3.3 Configuration C: always writeable—(N, R, W) = (3, 1, 1)

- **Math:** 1 + 1 = 2 < 3. No overlap.
- **Behavior:** writes are instant—a single "got it" suffices—and reads are instant too.
- **Cost:** eventual consistency. Consider:

- A user adds an iPad (written to node A).
- The user immediately refreshes the page (read served by node B).
- Node B has not yet received the replication.
- *Result:* the user sees an empty cart.

The shopping cart is the canonical "always writeable" application: it must never reject an "add to cart," even during failures. The original Dynamo system does not pin the cart to a specific (N, R, W) triple. What it does is that applications needing the highest availability can push W all the way down to 1, and that the cart relies on **business-logic reconciliation**—merging divergent versions of a customer's cart—rather than on strong read-time consistency. The lesson to carry forward is the direction of the choice, not a magic triple: Amazon prioritized "never miss an add to cart" over "always show the latest state in the next 200 milliseconds." A daring choice for 2007. With configuration C, there is also a danger of data loss if the single node where the write happened fails before replication occurs.

> **Aside: Instance-Level vs. Per-Request Tuning**
>
> In the original Dynamo design, N, R, and W were fixed at the instance level: a team configured the cluster once, and every request obeyed those values. Later architectures in the same lineage (notably Apache Cassandra) let engineers pass the consistency level on each individual get and put, so a single database can serve both high-speed and high-consistency queries at once. This book's talk of "clients choosing" N, R, and W refers to that later capability. The original 2007 Dynamo could not do this.

5.4 The Critical Twist: "Sloppy" Quorum

Most explanations stop at W = 1. But there is one more step into the "dark side" of availability—and it is the step that makes Dynamo genuinely always writeable.

A **strict quorum** insists on votes from the designated owners of the key. Suppose N = 3 and the preference list for our key is (A, B, C):

- *Scenario:* A is alive; B and C are down.
- *Result:* with W = 2 we can collect only one vote. The write fails, and the customer cannot buy the item.

A **sloppy quorum** refuses to fail. Instead of demanding the designated owners, it performs the operation on the **first N healthy nodes from the**

preference list—walking further around the ring, past the down owners, until it finds N reachable homes (Figure 5.5):

- *Scenario:* B and C are down, so the coordinator on A walks clockwise and enlists the next healthy nodes, D and E.
- *Result:* the write succeeds. The data lands on A, D, and E—still N = 3 durable copies.

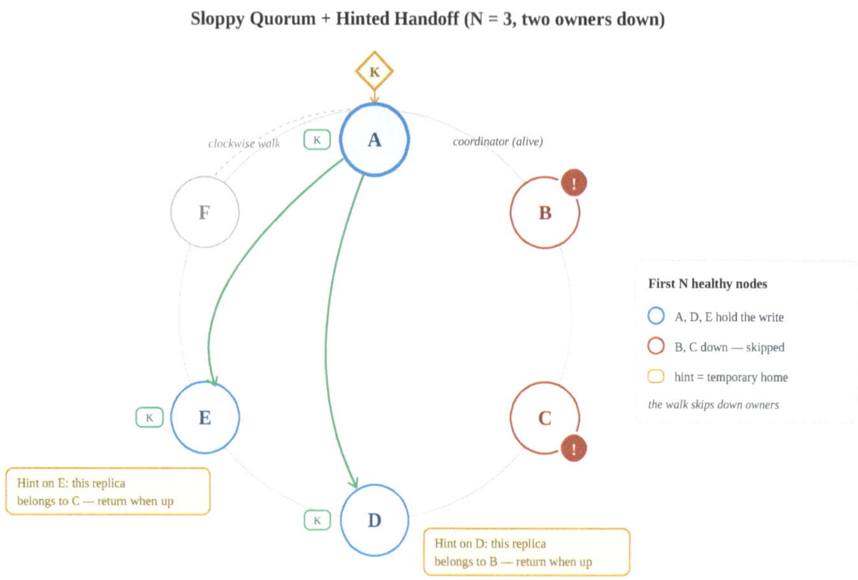

Figure 5.5 **Sloppy Quorum and Hinted Handoff.** With owners B and C down, the coordinator walks past them and stores the N = 3 copies on the first healthy nodes—A, D, and E. D and E tag their copies with a hint naming the rightful owner, so the data can be handed back once B and C recover.

Hinted handoff. Nodes D and E know they are not the true owners of this key. Each stores its copy in a separate local database with a hint in the metadata— effectively a sticky note: *"This replica really belongs to B"* (and on E, *"...to C"*). That separate store is scanned periodically; the moment D detects that B has recovered, it ships the replica back to B and may then drop its own copy—without ever reducing the total number of replicas in the system. This is how we preserve durability and availability through a transient outage.

There is a cost to leaning on this too heavily. If many nodes across the ring are simultaneously holding hinted data for absent owners, they accumulate keys that do not belong to them and must eventually drain that data back to its rightful homes—work that can degrade the cluster if the churn is large or prolonged.

How far can availability go? With W = 1, a write is accepted as long as a single node can durably store it, so the write is rejected *only* if every node in the system is unavailable. In practice, most Amazon services in production chose a higher W to get stronger durability—but the knob goes all the way to 1 when availability is paramount.

5.5 Summary

By combining a **sloppy quorum** with a low **W** (down to W = 1), an online vendor reaches its goal: **zero-downtime writes**—the store accepts an order as long as any node is up.

But speed has a price. If anyone may write anywhere without waiting for agreement, you will eventually produce **conflicts**:

- Node A thinks the cart holds an iPad.
- Node B thinks it holds a Kindle.
- Node C thinks it is empty.

These divergences usually arise from network or node failures. When the failure heals and the nodes finally compare notes, who wins?

We cannot simply trust wall-clock timestamps to decide. Physical clocks on different machines drift out of sync—routinely, by tens or hundreds of milliseconds, with no malfunction involved—and that drift alone is enough to make "latest timestamp wins" pick the *wrong* write, even when the two writes were not concurrent at all and a true order existed.

Concretely: suppose a customer adds an iPad to their cart, then, ten seconds later, adds a Kindle to the same cart—two real, sequential actions, iPad first. The iPad write is coordinated by node A, whose clock is accurate. The Kindle write is coordinated by node B, whose clock happens to be running fifteen seconds behind real time. Node B stamps the Kindle write using its own (slow) clock, so on paper that write appears to have happened *before* the iPad write, even though in reality it came ten seconds *after* it. When the replicas later reconcile, last-write-wins compares the two timestamps the only way it knows how—numerically—and keeps the iPad write as the "later" one. The Kindle add, the customer's true final action, is silently discarded. Nothing about the request signals an error: the write succeeds, and the cart is simply wrong afterward.

This is not a contrived edge case: clock drift of tens to hundreds of milliseconds between machines is routine even with time-synchronization protocols running. It takes nothing more exotic than an ordinary clock running a little slow.

(Dynamo *does* offer a last-write-wins, timestamp-based mode, and some services—such as session storage—happily accept this risk. But for the shopping cart, where an "add to cart" must never be lost, silently dropping a legitimate write is unacceptable.) What the cart needs is a way to track the *causal history* of each version, so the system can tell a true overwrite from a genuine conflict without leaning on clocks at all. That mechanism is the **vector clock** (more precisely, the *version vector*), and it is where we turn next in Chapter 7 after a short detour in Chapter 6.

Before we tackle conflicts head-on, we first explain how the system cleans up the mess that sloppy quorum leaves behind—using hinted handoff and Merkle trees. In a distributed key-value store, failures are not exceptions; they are the norm. Chapter 6 details exactly how the system repairs itself when components fail.

References

- *DeCandia, G., et al., "Dynamo: Amazon's Highly Available Key-Value Store," ACM SOSP, 2007. §4.5 (Execution of get() and put() Operations), §4.6 (Handling Failures: Hinted Handoff), §5 (Implementation, the read-repair mechanism), §6 (Experiences & Lessons Learned, including the "high performance read engine" configuration).*
- *Attiya, H., Bar-Noy, A., and Dolev, D., "Sharing Memory Robustly in Message-Passing Systems," Journal of the ACM, 1995. (The ABD construction, mentioned as a contrast to Dynamo's best-effort consistency.)*

CHAPTER 6

Self-Healing (Handling Failures)

In a large cluster, something is always broken. Hard drives fail, network switches reboot, someone trips over a power cable, and configuration errors—most of them human in origin—quietly chip away at the reliability of any service. At Amazon scale, failure is not an exception; it is the normal operating condition.

If our key-value store needed a human every time a server faltered, a hyperscaler would have to hire an army of sysadmins. Instead, the system is designed to be **self-healing**. To repair itself efficiently, it first distinguishes between two kinds of trouble:

- **Transient failures (the blip):** a node is unresponsive for a few minutes—a reboot, a brief network hiccup.
- **Longer or permanent failures (the crash):** a node is gone for hours, or its hardware is destroyed and replaced with an empty machine.

Each calls for a completely different repair strategy. But here is the catch we will keep circling back to: *how does a node tell the two apart?* Hold that question—we answer it at the end of the chapter.

6.1 Transient Failures: Hinted Handoff

Hinted handoff is the mechanism behind the **sloppy quorum** from Chapter 5. It keeps the system **available** during short outages.

The scenario. A write for a shopping cart is meant for **Node A**, but A is overloaded or rebooting.

The solution. Rather than fail the write—which loses a sale—the coordinator walks the preference list and hands the write to the next *healthy* node clockwise on the ring, say **Node D**. This is exactly the sloppy quorum at work: the write lands on the first N healthy nodes, which need not be the first N nodes encountered while walking the ring.

Node D accepts the write but knows it is not the rightful owner. It stores the data in a **separate, temporary store** and attaches a piece of metadata—a *hint*—recording who the data really belongs to: "Target: Node A. Key: user_101."

The recovery. Node D periodically scans that temporary store and checks whether Node A has come back. The moment A is reachable again, D delivers the held data. Once A acknowledges receipt, D deletes its local copy—and crucially, this deletion does **not** reduce the total number of replicas in the system, because A now holds the data it was always meant to.

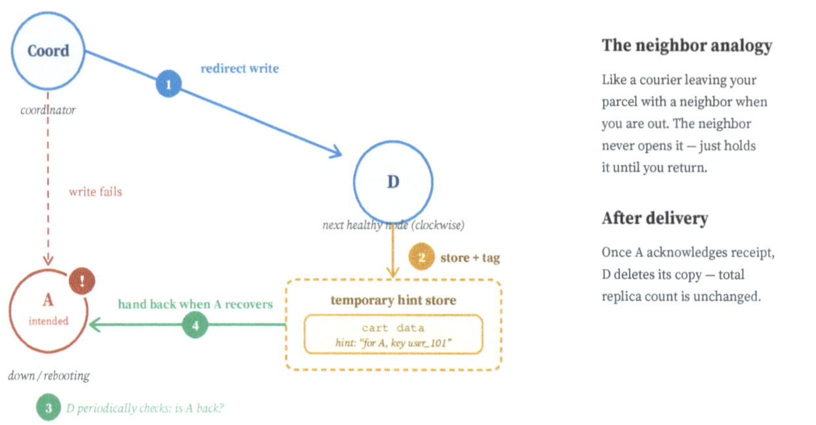

Figure 6.1 **Hinted Handoff.** A write meant for the down node A is redirected to healthy node D, which holds it with a hint. When A recovers, D hands the data back and deletes its copy—like a courier leaving a parcel with a neighbor.

6.2 Longer / Permanent Failures: Anti-Entropy

Hinted handoff shines for short blips. But what if Node A is down for six hours?

- The hints accumulating on Node D might expire or overflow.
- Worse, A might have suffered a total disk failure and come back as a completely empty server.

Either way, we need a way to bring A back into sync with B and C—both nodes holding copies of A's key range—and recover the data it missed. This background reconciliation is called **anti-entropy**—the background process that counters replica drift.

Read repair (introduced in Chapter 5) covers one piece of this puzzle: when a quorum read finds a stale replica, it patches it on the spot. But read repair only helps keys that somebody happens to read. Keys that sit unread for days—less popular data, recently restored partitions—stay stale until something else notices them. That "something else" is anti-entropy: a systematic background scan that finds and fixes divergence even on data nobody is actively reading.

The challenge. A was offline for hours while B (a replica of node A) kept accepting writes (let's assume changed values to the same keys). Both nodes now hold roughly 100 GB, but A's copy is stale.

The naive approach. B ships its entire 100 GB to A to guarantee they match.

The problem. That obliterates network bandwidth. Out of ten million keys, perhaps only 500 changed during the outage. Moving 100 GB to fix 500 keys is enormous waste.

The goal. We want A and B to compare two large databases over the network, isolate exactly which ~500 keys differ, and transfer only those. (The one unavoidable exception: if A returns with a fresh, empty disk, B simply has to send everything.)

6.3 The Magic Tool: Merkle Trees

We solve this with Merkle trees (hash trees)—a structure worth knowing in its own right, built up from scratch in appendix A. The short version: it is built bottom-up:

- **Leaves:** the hash of each key's stored value.
- **Branches:** each parent is the hash of its children's hashes.
- **Root:** a single root hash that fingerprints the entire key range.

> **Aside: A Note on Precision**
>
> Picturing one leaf per key keeps the diagram simple, but real implementations give each leaf a small *range* of keys, not a single key. That detail is exactly what keeps two replicas' trees identically shaped and comparable—and it's why an absent key is never a problem. Appendix A develops the structure properly, with worked shopping-cart examples; this chapter keeps the per-key view for intuition.

How syncing works. Stale Node A and healthy Node B compare notes top-down, descending only where they disagree:

- **Compare roots.** A says XYZ; B says ABC. Mismatch—the ranges differ somewhere.

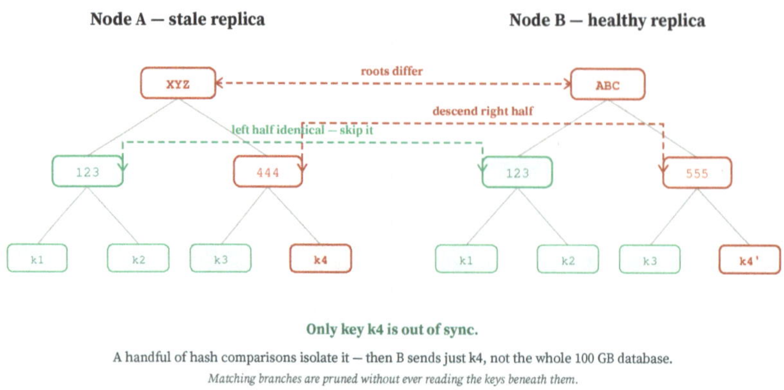

Figure 6.2 **Anti-entropy with Merkle trees.** Mismatched roots trigger a top-down comparison; matching branches (green) are pruned, divergent ones (red) are explored. A few hash exchanges isolate the single out-of-sync key, which is the only data actually transferred.

- **Compare the next level.** Left-branch hashes match (123 = 123)—the entire left half is identical and can be skipped without ever reading the keys beneath it. The right branch differs ($444 \neq 555$)—dig there.
- **Descend until the leaves.** They keep splitting the disagreement until they isolate the exact differing keys.

Bandwidth saved. Instead of 100 GB, the two nodes trade a handful of tiny hashes and then move only the specific keys that differ. Each matching branch prunes away half the remaining work.

Deep Dive: Sparse vs. dense divergence. Merkle trees are tuned for **sparse** differences—finding a needle in a haystack with little effort. The right trigger for each strategy is *how much* of the key space has drifted, not how long the node was down:

- **Few keys changed** (divergence below a threshold): Merkle trees shine. A handful of hash comparisons locates the mismatched leaves; only those keys are transferred.
- **Many keys changed** (divergence above a threshold): the back-and-forth hash comparison generates more overhead than it saves. Modern systems detect this condition and simply **bypass the Merkle tree**, triggering a **bulk transfer**—streaming the raw key-value data directly.

Note: the Dynamo system uses Merkle-tree anti-entropy; the bulk-transfer fallback above is standard practice in Dynamo’s descendants (e.g., Cassandra), included here as practical context.

6.4 The “Partitioning Strategy” Nuance

Recall the three ring-placement strategies from Chapter 2. The choice of strategy has a direct, and often overlooked, effect on Merkle trees.

- **The dependency:** a Merkle tree is computed over the keys in a specific range.
- **The flaw of Strategy 1 (random tokens):** when a node joined or left, key ranges shifted and keys migrated between nodes. The affected Merkle tree became invalid instantly, forcing a recalculation from scratch—expensive on a busy production node.
- **The fix (fixed partitions):** Strategy 2 introduced fixed partition slots, and Strategy 3—the scheme Dynamo actually runs—keeps them. Each partition carries its own Merkle tree. Hand a partition to another node and its tree travels with it as a file. No recalculation.

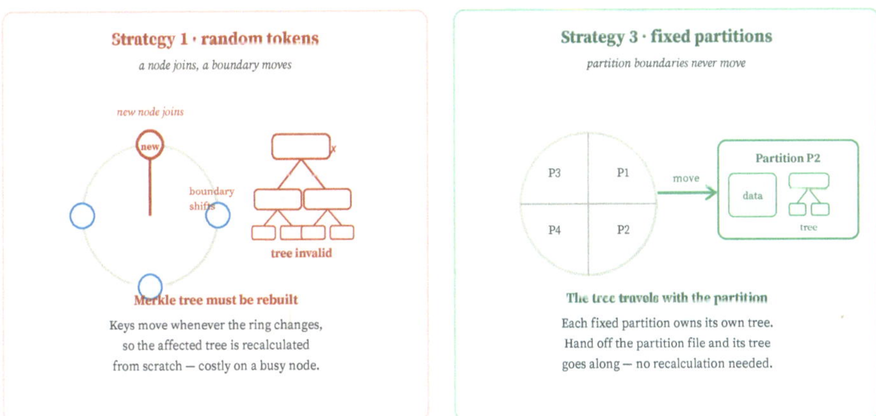

Figure 6.3 **Why fixed partitions matter for repair.** Under random tokens, a ring change shifts boundaries and invalidates the Merkle tree. Under fixed partitions, each partition owns a tree that moves with it—the production scheme avoids costly rebuilds.

Deep Dive: Parallel repair across virtual nodes. Remember that one physical node hosts many virtual nodes, each responsible for different partitions on the ring. If a physical machine restarts with a fresh disk, the replica virtual nodes—scattered across many other physical servers—can detect the missing data using their own Merkle trees **in parallel** and stream it to the new node simultaneously. The work of detecting and repairing is spread across many peers instead of burdening one. Modern data-center fabrics (for example, Clos (pronounced "Klo") topologies) provide many redundant paths, so data can arrive from multiple sources over multiple routes at once. The recovering node controls the *ingestion* rate by limiting how many peers send to it at any moment.

6.5 Using Merkle Trees on a Busy Node

If Merkle trees are constantly summarizing live key-value data, what happens when a write lands *mid-sync*? If the hashes shift while we are reading them, the comparison is worthless.

So systems rarely build Merkle trees on live, mutating data. They build them on **snapshots**. Before a sync, the node freezes a read-only view of its stored key-value data, builds the tree on that frozen view, and lets live traffic continue writing to new files in the background. Because new writes go to separate, active files while the snapshot remains untouched, the database continues serving reads and writes throughout the entire sync – it is never locked to repair itself.

6.5.1 The Solution: Point-in-Time Snapshots

Rather than read live data, the node leans on its storage engine to provide a static, read-only view of the data as of a specific millisecond. Here is the mechanism, step by step:

- **The snapshot command.** When A and B agree to run an anti-entropy sync, neither starts comparing immediately. Each first asks its local storage engine for a snapshot—a freeze of the key-value state at that instant.
- **Copy-on-write (or LSM trees).** Because modern engines use multi-version concurrency control (MVCC) or log-structured merge (LSM) trees, taking a snapshot is nearly instantaneous and initially costs almost no extra storage. The engine simply draws a line in the sand: any write after 12:00:00.000 goes into new files; the old files become immutable.
- **Build the tree on frozen data.** A and B compute their Merkle trees against these read-only snapshots. Because the underlying data cannot change, the hashes are stable, and the two nodes can take as long as they need to traverse the tree, find mismatches, and ship the missing keys.

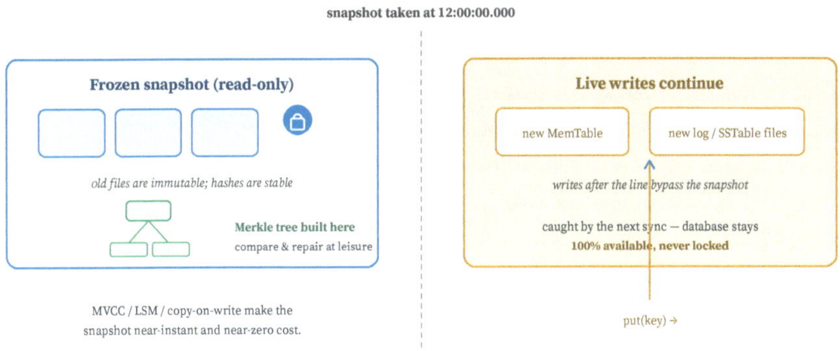

Figure 6.4 **Repairing without locking.** The Merkle tree is built on an immutable point-in-time snapshot while live writes flow into new files. MVCC/LSM make the snapshot near-instant, so the node stays fully available throughout the sync.

- **Live traffic flows uninterrupted.** Meanwhile the database stays 100% available. New `put(key)` writes land in the active memory buffer (MemTable) or a new log file, bypassing the frozen snapshot. They will be picked up by the *next* scheduled sync.

Note: snapshotting, MVCC/LSM internals, and distributed-snapshot coordination are not part of the original 2007 Dynamo design. They are how production storage engines realize anti-entropy safely, included here to connect Dynamo's idea to practice.

A correctness caveat. Taking coordinated snapshots across multiple nodes needs care: if A freezes its view at 12:00:00.000 but B freezes at 12:00:00.050, are they truly comparing the same moment? Classic distributed-snapshot algorithms such as *Chandy–Lamport* address exactly this—each node takes a local snapshot and propagates "marker" messages through communication channels to capture a globally consistent cut of the system state, without stopping the world. Chandy–Lamport is one tool among several for getting this right.

6.5.2 Deep Dive: Distinguishing Transient and Permanent Failures

Now we can answer the question from the opening. **A node cannot mathematically prove whether a peer is briefly disconnected, merely slow, or unreachable.** A network timeout looks identical to a dead logic board. So the architecture never tries to guess up front—it uses a **time-based escalation**:

- **Assume transient (hinted handoff).** When a write to a peer times out, treat it as a blip and stash the data with a hint.
- **The tipping point (run out of patience).** A node cannot hold hints forever; another node's data would eventually fill its storage and threaten its own stability. A configured time-to-live—for example, 24 hours—or a separate storage-size cap limits this. Past the threshold, the system stops treating the failure as a quick blip. A well-run cluster's monitoring system should alert the operator when hints approach these limits, so the situation is addressed before data is lost.
- **The long game (anti-entropy).** If the missing node finally returns after, say, three days, it has missed thousands of writes. It now *pulls* what it missed by comparing Merkle trees with its replica peers (or bulk-copying if divergence exceeds the threshold described above).
- **The final verdict (explicit permanent death).** From the system's point of view, a node is never truly dead until the control plane says so. If hardware is destroyed, peers simply keep noticing it is unreachable; it is declared dead only when an administrator (or an orchestration tool) issues a command to **remove it from the ring**. Gossip then spreads the news—discard its token, neighbors expand to cover its territory.

On the hinted data itself: if a returning node B also has hints waiting for it on a peer, and B did *not* start from an empty disk, it is often best to fold in that fresh hinted data first and only then run the Merkle-tree comparison against its peers.

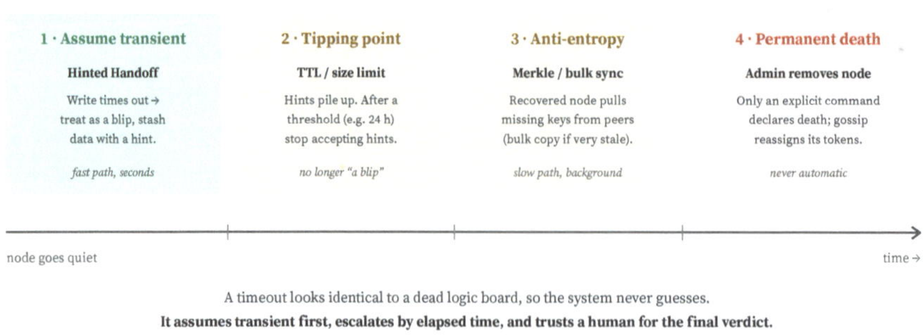

Figure 6.5 **The failure-escalation ladder.** Because a timeout is indistinguishable from a dead logic board, the system assumes transient first and escalates by elapsed time. Only an explicit administrative removal declares a node permanently dead.

In summary: the system does not know which failure occurred, so it assumes every failure is transient at first, using lightweight 'sticky notes' to hold data temporarily. Only when a node stays gone for a long time—or an administrator explicitly removes it—does it deploy the heavy machinery for a permanent repair. Hinted handoff is the **fast path** for common transient failures; Merkle trees (with bulk transfer as backstop) are the **slow path** for everything else: permanent failures, lost hints, and silent corruption. Merkle trees excel when differences are sparse; when a database is wildly out of sync, a bulk copy wins.

6.6 Summary

Our key-value store stays safe through a two-tiered repair system:

- **Hinted handoff** keeps the system writable through short blips.
- **Merkle-tree anti-entropy** efficiently repairs replicas after longer crashes.

But all this shuffling of data introduces our next challenge:

- Hinted handoff lets Node D accept a write meant for Node A.
- Meanwhile, Node B might accept a different write for the same key.
- Now two valid, divergent versions of the same shopping cart are loose on the network.

When the system heals, those two versions meet. Who wins? The database cannot decide on its own—and timestamps cannot be trusted to order the writes. It needs a principled way to describe the conflict to the application.

In the next chapter, we explore why wall-clock based timestamps are dangerous, and how **version vectors** (the precise cousin of the vector clock) let us detect and merge conflicting histories. This is the cost of the high availability we bought in Chapter 5.

References

- *DeCandia, G., et al., "Dynamo: Amazon's Highly Available Key-Value Store," ACM SOSP, 2007. §4.6 (Handling Failures: Hinted Handoff), §4.7 (Handling Permanent Failures: Replica Synchronization, including Merkle-tree anti-entropy).*
- *Merkle, R.C., "A Digital Signature Based on a Conventional Encryption Function," Advances in Cryptology — CRYPTO '87, LNCS Vol. 293, 1988, pp. 369–378. (Introduces the hash tree structure used in anti-entropy repair.)*
- *Chandy, K.M. and Lamport, L., "Distributed Snapshots: Determining Global States of Distributed Systems," ACM Transactions on Computer Systems, 3(1), 1985. (The foundational algorithm for capturing consistent global snapshots without stopping the system.)*

CHAPTER 7

When Time Lies (Conflict Resolution)

In Chapter 5 we made our database "Always Writable" by combining a sloppy quorum with W = 1: a write succeeds on the first available healthy node, even during a partition. That means a user can modify their shopping cart even when the network is broken and servers cannot talk to one another.

Network splits are not hypothetical. A landmark study of tens of geographically distributed production datacenters found link and device failures occurring regularly, with network redundancy only 40% effective at reducing their median impact (Gill et al., SIGCOMM 2011). Under exactly these conditions, the "Always Writable" guarantee creates a dangerous side effect: **divergence.**

Suppose the network is split. A user adds an **iPad** on Server A, and ten seconds later adds an **Apple Pencil** on Server B:

- Server A has: [iPad]
- Server B has: [Apple Pencil]

When the network heals, the database is faced with two carts:

- Merge them into [iPad, Apple Pencil]—correct.

Or apply **"Last-Writer-Wins"** by timestamp. LWW does not know which write actually happened later in the real world—it only compares *clock values*. If Server A's clock happens to be running ahead of Server B's, the iPad's timestamp can beat the Pencil's even though the Pencil was added second. The Apple Pencil is silently dropped—the data loss runs in whichever direction the clock skew happens to point.

> **Aside: Last-Writer-Wins—Dangerous by Default, Safe by Choice**
>
> LWW feels natural to us humans, because we carry a single shared

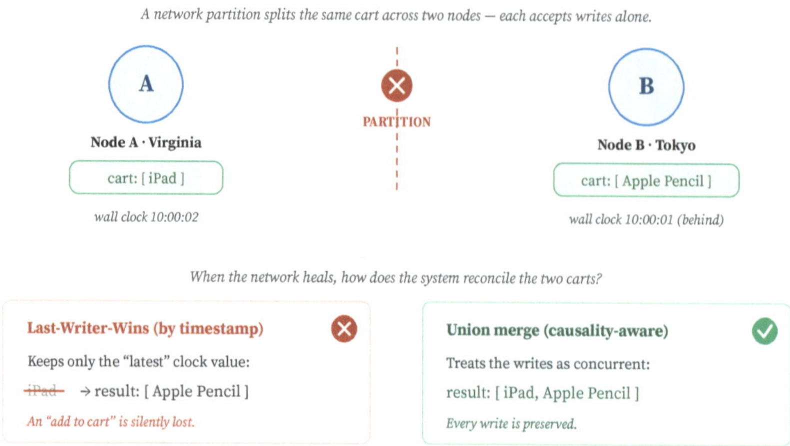

Figure 7.1 **The Divergence Problem and the Last-Writer-Wins Trap.** A network partition lets the same cart diverge across two nodes. Node A's clock is running ahead, so choosing the "latest" write by timestamp keeps the iPad and silently drops the Apple Pencil—even though the Pencil was added second in the real world. A causality-aware union keeps every "add to cart."

> notion of time through our daily lives. But computers do not. Because clocks drift, LWW can lose data and produce confusing behaviour. The system's state no longer matches the customer's reality.
> That said, LWW is not only a cautionary tale. Dynamo supports *timestamp-based reconciliation* as an opt-in mode: when an application chooses it, Dynamo keeps the version with the largest **physical** timestamp. The customer-session service uses exactly this. What makes it tolerable there is the kind of data: a session blob is overwrite-friendly. If clock skew causes an older session to win on timestamp, the worst outcome is that the user re-authenticates or loses a minor recent preference—session state self-corrects at the next interaction. A cart is the opposite: a silently dropped "add to cart" is an unrecoverable business event. And notice the timestamp is **physical, not logical**—which is exactly why clock skew can let an older write win. A logical clock cannot rescue LWW here: concurrent versions are *incomparable*, so any winner-takes-all rule must fall back to a *total* order such as wall-clock time. We build this argument from first principles in appendix B.

To prevent data loss, we need a way to understand the **causal history** of the data—to know whether the Pencil was added *after* the iPad (a sequence) or *independently* of it (concurrency).

7.1 Why Timestamps Are a Lie

Your instinct is to trust the system clock:

- "Write A happened at 10:00:01."
- "Write B happened at 10:00:02."
- Therefore B is newer.

In a distributed system, **this inference can be wrong.** Server clocks drift. Server A might be in Virginia and Server B in Tokyo. Even with NTP (Network Time Protocol), their clocks can be off by tens of milliseconds—and in a high-speed system, that is a large margin. You cannot trust wall-clock time to order events.

We need a **logical clock** instead. For our purposes we only care about tracking updates to the replicas of a single object, not every event in the system. So rather than full *vector clocks* we will use *version vectors*. (We will draw out the difference between the two once we have seen one in action.)

> **Aside: Time Synchronization Is Hard (Post-2007 Context)**
>
> We cannot synchronize two clocks with infinite precision. What we can do is bound the drift between them. Google's Spanner does exactly this through its TrueTime API—a system that postdates Dynamo (2007) and is offered here as descendant-systems context. To sidestep the problem entirely, Leslie Lamport invented Lamport clocks, later generalized to vector clocks. These are logical "clocks": they do not tell wall-clock time; they let us infer a partial ordering of events.

7.2 What Is a Version Vector?

A version vector is a small piece of metadata attached to every object (for us, every key). It is a list of **(Node, Counter)** pairs:

```
Version Vector:  [Node_A: 1, Node_B: 2]
```

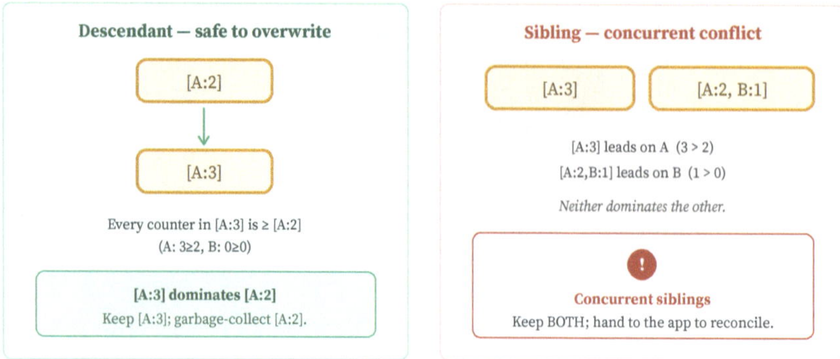

Figure 7.2 **Descendant vs. Sibling.** Left: one clock dominates the other at every node, so it is a true descendant and safely overwrites. Right: each clock leads on a different node, so the versions are concurrent siblings and both survive.

It tells a story: *"this version of the object has been updated once by Node A and twice by Node B."*

7.3 The Rules of Dominance

To decide whether version X is newer than version Y, we compare their counters node by node.

- **Descendant (newer):** if X's counter is greater-than-or-equal-to Y's for *every* node—treating any node *absent* from a logical clock as 0—and strictly greater for at least one, then X is a descendant of Y. X already contains Y's history, so Y can be safely overwritten. Dynamo calls this case **syntactic reconciliation**: the system resolves it on its own, from the logical clocks alone, with no help from the application.
- **Sibling (conflict):** if X has a higher counter for one node but Y has a higher counter for another, neither caused the other. They are *concurrent*—siblings—and both must be kept. Resolving *this* case needs help from the application—Dynamo's **semantic reconciliation**, which we walk through next.

7.4 The Life of a Shopping Cart (A Walkthrough)

Let us trace one cart through a network failure to watch version vectors do their work. The whole journey—from a single write to a clean reconciliation—is shown in Figure 7.3; the steps below narrate it.

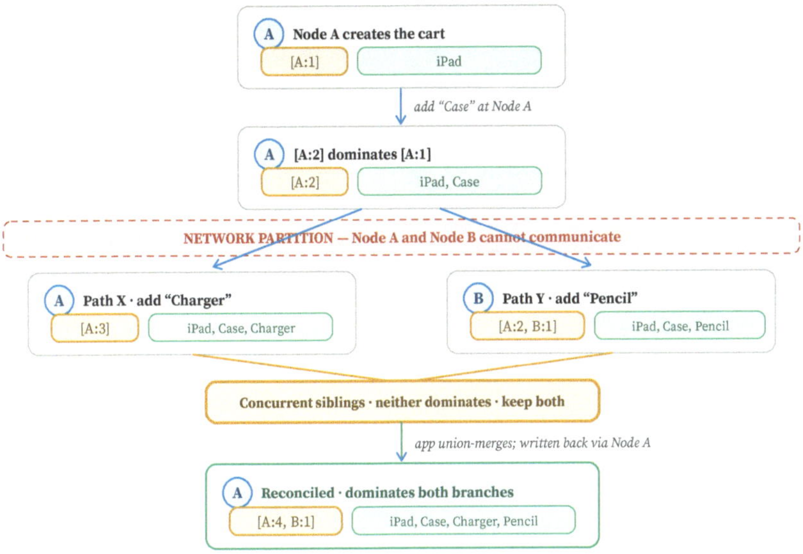

Figure 7.3 **The Life of a Shopping Cart.** A single object evolves from `[A:1]` to `[A:4, B:1]`. A partition forks it into two concurrent versions that the application later reconciles by union. (This mirrors Figure 3 of DeCandia et al. 2007, retold with the book's cart.)

7.4.1 Step 1 — Creation

The user adds an **iPad**. The request hits Node A, which creates the object and starts the clock.

- Data: [iPad]
- Clock: `[A:1]`

7.4.2 Step 2 — Sequential Update

The user adds a **Case**. The request hits Node A again, which increments its own counter.

- Data: [iPad, Case]
- Clock: `[A:2]`
- Logic: `[A:2]` dominates `[A:1]`; the old version is garbage-collected—*syntactic reconciliation*, resolved by the system alone.

7.4.3 Step 3 — The Network Partition (the split)

The network breaks. Node A and Node B (a replica of Node A) can no longer talk, and the user (or load balancer) is routed to different nodes on each side.

- **Path X (Node A is alive):** the user adds **Charger**. Node A updates locally—Data [iPad, Case, Charger], Clock `[A:3]`.
- **Path Y (Node A unreachable, routed to Node B):** the user adds **Pencil.** Node B reads the last version it has (`[A:2]`), adds its own counter—Data [iPad, Case, Pencil], Clock `[A:2, B:1]`.

7.4.4 Step 4 — The Read (conflict discovery)

The network heals and the user asks to view their cart. The coordinator reads from both nodes and compares the two clocks:

- Is `[A:3]` > `[A:2, B:1]`? No—A:3 > A:2, but X is missing B:1.
- Is `[A:2, B:1]` > `[A:3]`? No—B:1 is new, but A:2 < A:3.
- **Verdict:** the two versions are **siblings** (concurrent events).

7.4.5 Step 5 — Semantic Reconciliation

Unlike Step 2, this is not a case the clocks alone can settle. The database cannot resolve it on its own: it does not know whether the user deleted the Charger to add the Pencil, or wanted both. With no descendant on either side, *syntactic reconciliation* is not available, so it takes the only safe path—it hands both versions back to the client application for **semantic reconciliation.**

System: *"I have a conflict. Here are two carts. You fix it."*

- `[iPad, Case, Charger]`
- `[iPad, Case, Pencil]`

> **Aside: Git: The Same Conflict**
>
> This is the same situation you meet in Git: when it cannot merge two versions of a file automatically, it surfaces the conflict and asks a human to resolve it.

Different applications resolve such conflicts differently, and what is appropriate depends entirely on the use case. For a shopping cart, simply merging the two versions is reasonable—the user can always remove anything they did not want from the combined cart.

So the **client app** (the web / application server logic) performs a union:

- Merged data: [iPad, Case, Charger, Pencil]
- The client writes this merged object back to the database.
- The coordinator (say, Node A) updates the clock to record that it has now seen both histories—new clock `[A:4, B:1]`.

Now `[A:4, B:1]` dominates both previous versions. The conflict is resolved. On the next read that reaches Node B, **read repair** (Chapter 6) will detect its stale `[A:2, B:1]` copy and overwrite it with the merged `[A:4, B:1]` version, bringing all replicas back into sync.

> **Aside: Who Is the "Client"?**
>
> Many people picture the end user when they read "client." That is not what it means here. Client-server is a communication paradigm, and the same machine can act as a server in one exchange and a client in another. In this discussion the "client" is a web server talking to our key-value store's coordinator.

And if the user really did delete the Charger before adding the Pencil? The end user resolves it—by removing it again, or, if they were careless and placed the order, the unwanted item is returned or settled afterward. The lesson is the same: providing strong consistency here would have cost us availability. By design we tolerate brief inconsistency so that the customer's shopping experience never stops.

> **Aside: Vector Clocks vs. Version Vectors**
>
> You will find people debating whether what we just used is a *version vector* or a *vector clock*. Both terms refer to the same mathematical structure; the difference is scope. A vector clock tracks system-wide causality among events—one entry per process. A version vector tracks per-object causality among replica updates—one entry per replica. Dynamo's original design uses the term "vector clock" throughout; what it implements is, strictly speaking, a version vector. We derive all three concepts—Lamport clocks, vector clocks, and version vectors—from first principles, with worked examples, in appendix B.

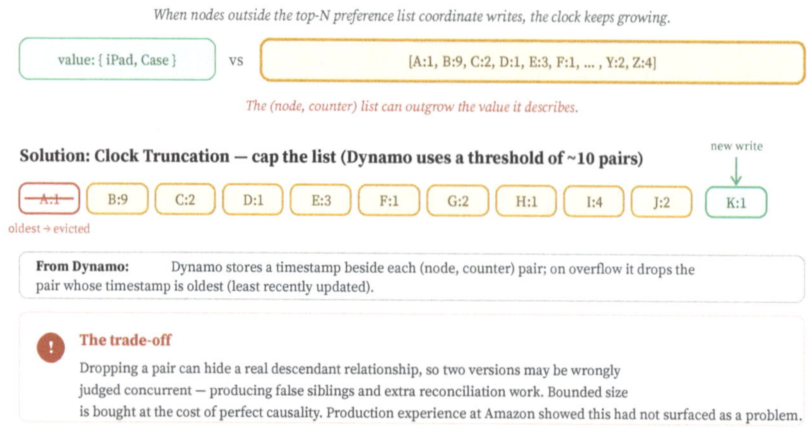

Figure 7.4 **The Dark Side: Clock Truncation.** When out-of-preference-list nodes coordinate writes, the version vector grows until it can dwarf the data. Dynamo caps it by evicting the pair with the oldest stored timestamp—trading perfect causality for bounded size.

7.5 The "Dark Side": Clock Truncation

Version vectors have a practical weakness: the set of nodes that touch an object can grow over time. In normal operation this is not a problem, because writes are coordinated by one of the top-N nodes in the preference list. But during network partitions or multiple failures—exactly the conditions *sloppy quorum* and *hinted handoff* are built for—writes are coordinated by nodes *outside* the top N. If a long-lived cart is handled by hundreds of such nodes over its lifetime, the clock string balloons:

```
[A:1, B:9, C:2, D:1, ... , Z:4]
```

The metadata can eventually exceed the *data* it describes.

Solution—clock truncation. Dynamo caps the list at a threshold (about 10 pairs). To know which pair is "oldest," Dynamo stores a *timestamp* alongside each (node, counter) pair, recording the last time that node updated the item. When the list overflows, the pair with the oldest timestamp is dropped to make room for the new one.

You might wonder whether using physical timestamps here reintroduces the clock-skew hazard we warned against earlier. The risk is categorically different. LWW uses timestamps to pick a *data winner*, which can silently discard a write. Truncation uses timestamps only to rank *metadata entries* for eviction; no write is ever discarded. If clock skew causes the "wrong" pair to be dropped, the worst outcome is a false sibling—the system surfaces a conflict to the application that the logical clocks could have resolved automatically. The application still gets to merge the versions; no data is lost silently. That asymmetry—unnecessary reconciliation versus invisible data loss—is why the system uses physical timestamps here despite avoiding them for data ordering.

- **The risk:** removing a pair means losing causal history. The system may then classify two versions as siblings when one actually dominated the other.
- **The trade-off:** perfect conflict resolution versus bounded storage and the cost of extra reconciliations. An operator can tune how long causal chains are allowed to grow. Production experience at Amazon showed this truncation had not surfaced as a problem.

7.6 Summary

Version vectors let our key-value store honor the "Always Writable" promise without losing data.

- **Traditional DB:** "I cannot accept this write because I cannot lock the row." (Downtime.)
- **Our key-value store:** "I will accept this write, but you—the application, or the end user in rare cases—may have to clean up a mess later." (Complexity.)

That is the bargain: it shifts complexity from the database operator to the application developer. It is the price of scale.

With the architecture of our key-value store complete, we turn to the final layer of polish: how "smart clients" and a focus on P99 latency make the store fast enough to live under a strict service-level agreement. Chapter 8 moves from architecture to engineering—tuning the engine for production.

References

- *DeCandia, G., et al., "Dynamo: Amazon's Highly Available Key-Value Store," ACM SOSP, 2007. §4.4 (Data Versioning: version vectors, syntactic vs. semantic reconciliation, and clock truncation).*
- *Gill, P., Jain, N., and Nagappan, N., "Understanding Network Failures in Data Centers: Measurement, Analysis, and Implications," ACM SIGCOMM, 2011, pp. 350–361. (First large-scale measurement of datacenter network failures across tens of geographically distributed facilities; network redundancy is only 40% effective at reducing the median impact of failure.)*

- *Corbett, J.C., et al., "Spanner: Google's Globally Distributed Database," USENIX OSDI, 2012. (Introduces TrueTime, a bounded clock-uncertainty API that sidesteps NTP drift by tracking worst-case clock skew directly; cited here as post-2007 descendant-systems context.)*

CHAPTER 8

Chasing the Tail (Performance Optimizations)

We have built a key-value store that is scalable (add or remove virtual nodes on the Ring), decentralized (Gossip), durable (Replication), and resilient (Self-Healing). But is it fast in real use?

From Chapter 1, we have known we were studying Dynamo, and throughout—partitioning, gossip, replication, quorums, failure-handling, conflict resolution—our method has been to derive each design choice from first principles rather than accept it on faith. That method serves well when the question is *why*. It runs into a wall when the question is *how much*. Explaining why the Smart Client eliminates an extra network hop is pure reasoning; measuring how many milliseconds that hop actually costs requires a production system running at Amazon-scale traffic. For that, we draw directly on the source: Amazon's engineers published detailed performance data from Dynamo's peak December 2006 shopping season, and in this chapter we learn from their measurements.

In production, two performance problems dominate:

- **The extra hop.** A request routed through a load balancer often lands on a node that does not own the key, forcing an extra forwarding step across the network.
- **The tail, not the average.** Mean latency looks fine, but a small fraction of customers—often those with the largest objects and longest histories—experience slow responses.

Dynamo's answers were two ideas that reshaped how the industry thinks about performance: **client-driven coordination** (which we will call the **Smart Client**) and a relentless focus on the **99.9th-percentile (P99.9) latency**.

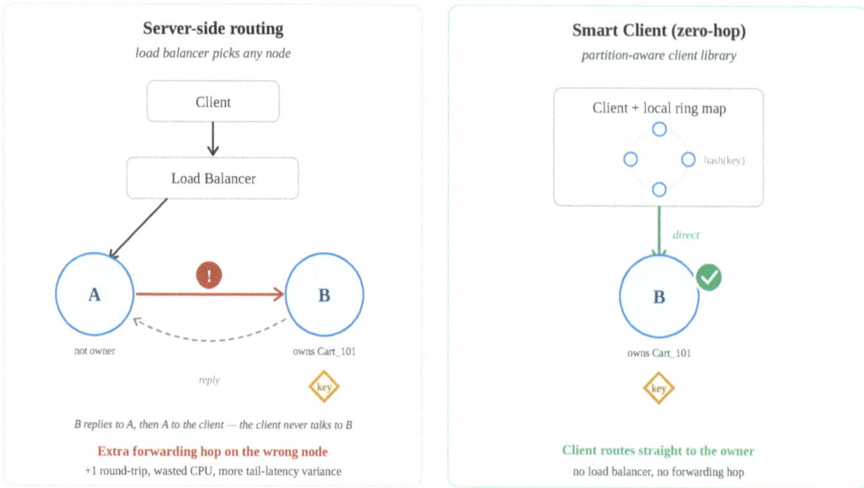

Figure 8.1 **Smart Routing Removes the Extra Hop.** Left: a load balancer drops the request on a random node, which must forward it to the owner. Right: a partition-aware client routes straight to the owner—a zero-hop path.

> **Aside: Who Are the "VIP" Customers?**
>
> Your most loyal, highest-spending customers often have the largest carts and the longest order histories. Both make their requests heavier to serve—more bytes to move, more personalization to compute—so they are exactly the users most likely to land in the slow tail. And for a service with billions of customers, a "small" tail is not small: if just 1% of a billion users see worse-than-average latency, that is 10 million people. This is why we measure the tail—the 90th, 99th, or 99.9th percentile—rather than trusting a comfortable P50.

8.1 The Bottleneck: Who Routes the Request?

The architecture we have described so far assumes a standard web setup: a client (web / application server) sends its request to a load balancer, which forwards it to some Dynamo node. Let's call this the generic-load-balancer strategy.

The problem is the extra hop. Suppose a client needs `Cart_101`:

- The load balancer picks a node—say Node A—based on load, not on who owns the key.
- Node A consults its hash ring and realizes it does not own `Cart_101`;

Node B does.

- Node A forwards the request to Node B, acting as a proxy.
- Node B does the work, replies to Node A, and Node A replies to the client.

This is simple—the client needs to know nothing about the database—but it is inefficient on two counts. You pay for an extra network round-trip whenever a request lands on the wrong node, and Node A burns CPU proxying data it does not own. And Node B cannot shortcut the return path by answering the client directly: the client only ever connected to Node A (through the load balancer) and has never heard of Node B, so the reply has to travel back the way it came. Because that forwarding step is variable, it inflates latency precisely at the high percentiles Dynamo cares about.

8.2 The Solution: The Smart Client

The fix is to remove the middleman by moving the routing logic out of the server and into the application—what Dynamo calls a partition-aware client library, and what we will call the **Smart Client**.

How it works (zero-hop routing):

- The client library, running inside the web / application server, periodically picks a random Dynamo node and downloads its current view of the membership state (the ring topology). In Dynamo this poll happens roughly every 10 seconds.
- When the application calls `put(key, value)` or `get(key)`, the library hashes the key locally and consults its copy of the ring to find the key's preference list—the nodes that own it.
- The library sends the request directly to the right node, skipping both the load balancer and the forwarding hop.

Dynamo describes itself as a **zero-hop DHT** (Distributed Hash Table): every node—and every smart client—holds enough routing information to reach the correct node directly, unlike multi-hop designs such as Chord or Pastry, whose extra hops add the variability that hurts the tail.

The trade-off—coupling.

- **Pro:** It is fast. Amazon measured the client-driven path shaving at least 30 ms off the 99.9th-percentile latency (and a few milliseconds off the average) versus routing through the load balancer.
- **Con:** The application now knows internal details of the database's topology. Upgrade the database and you may need to redeploy your

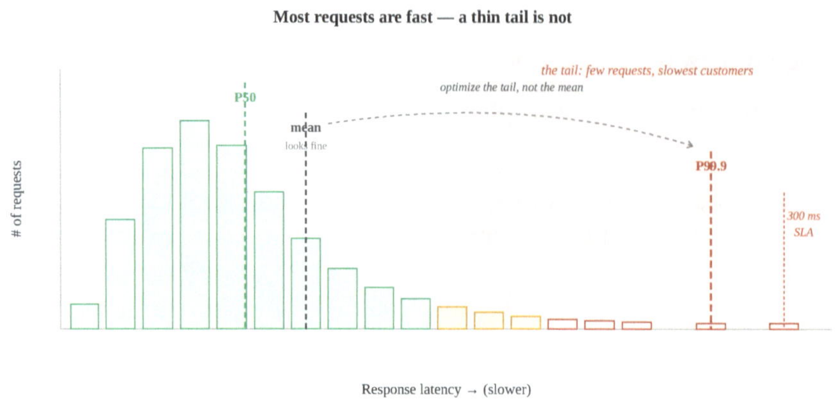

Figure 8.2 **The Mean Hides the Tail.** The bulk of requests are fast, so the average looks healthy. But the rare slow requests—the 99.9th percentile—are what the SLA must bound.

fleet of web / application servers to refresh the client library. Amazon accepted this operational coupling to win raw speed.

Why poll rather than push? A pull-based refresh scales to many clients with almost no per-client state on the servers. The cost is staleness: a client may hold an out-of-date map for up to one poll interval. If it notices the map is wrong—for instance, a node it expects is unreachable—it refreshes immediately.

A related server-side trick. *Among the top N nodes that could coordinate a write, Dynamo picks the one that replied fastest to the preceding read. This spreads coordination load, raises the odds of "read-your-writes," and trims variability at the 99.9th percentile.*

8.3 The Metric: Why "Average" Is No Longer Enough

Before Dynamo, most teams reported performance as an average or a median (P50): "our average response time is 200 ms." That single number hides the customers who suffer.

Consider 100 requests where 99 finish in 10 ms and one takes 20 seconds. The average is about 210 ms—and looks fine—yet one customer waited 20 seconds and is furious. Who is that customer? At Amazon, the slowest requests tend to come from users with the longest histories and largest objects: more personalization to compute, more bytes to move. In Dynamo, three things drive the tail: variability in request load, object sizes, and locality patterns—how "hot" a key is and whether it sits in a node's in-memory cache or requires a disk read. In other words, an SLA

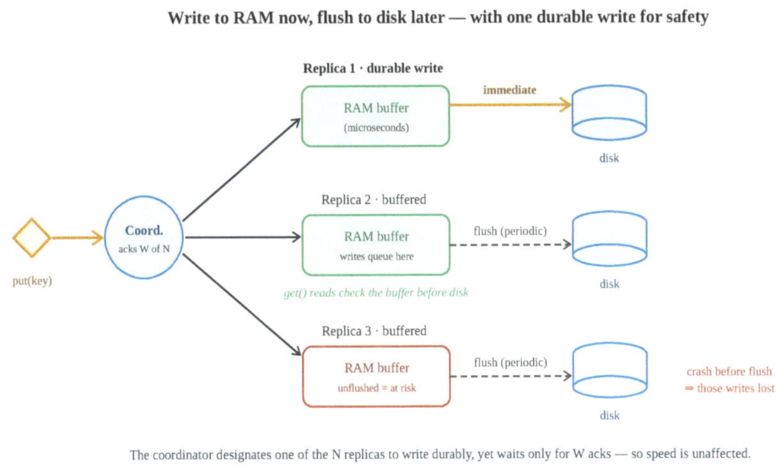

Figure 8.3 **Buffer in RAM, Flush Later—With One Durable Write.** Writes land in an in-memory buffer and a writer thread flushes them to disk; reads check the buffer first. To bound the durability risk, the coordinator has exactly one of the N replicas write straight to disk.

built on the average quietly lets down a business's heaviest, most engaged customers—exactly the people it can least afford to disappoint.

So Dynamo states its targets at the 99.9th percentile. A typical Dynamo SLA is that 99.9% of reads and writes complete within 300 ms at a defined peak load (Dynamo's own example is a peak of 500 requests per second). Engineers optimized the tail, not the mean—and chose 99.9% rather than, say, 99.99% after a cost-benefit analysis showed that the next "nine" got very expensive. In Dynamo's own measurements the 99.9th-percentile latencies ran around 200 ms, an order of magnitude *higher* than the averages.

Descendant-systems note. *This focus on tail latency has since become standard practice in site-reliability engineering at companies like Google, Netflix, and Uber; "average response time" is now widely treated as a vanity metric.*

8.4 Tuning the Engine: The Write Buffer

Even with routing fixed, individual nodes must keep up. On the commodity hardware Dynamo runs on, writes always hit disk, and a write is only as fast as the slowest of the W replicas that must acknowledge it. In 2007 that meant a rotating disk whose head must physically seek—slow, and a major source of tail latency.

For services that needed still-lower latency, Dynamo offered to trade a little durability for speed. Each storage node keeps an object buffer in main memory:

- A write lands in the in-memory buffer first (microseconds) and is acknowledged.
- A background writer thread periodically flushes the buffer to disk (milliseconds).
- A read checks the buffer first; if the key is present, it is served from memory without touching the storage engine.

For a buffer of just a thousand objects, this cut the 99.9th-percentile latency by a factor of five during peak traffic and smoothed the higher percentiles.

The risk, and the real mitigation. If a node crashes before its buffer flushes, those queued writes are lost. Dynamo's fix is specific and worth getting right: the coordinator designates one of the N replicas to perform a "durable write"—that replica writes straight to disk rather than buffering.

Why doesn't that disk write slow the whole operation down? The coordinator sends the write to all N replicas *simultaneously*, then waits for whichever W of them respond first. The buffered replicas write only to RAM and respond in microseconds; the durable-write replica writes to disk and takes a few milliseconds longer. Because W is typically less than N (e.g., $W = 2$ out of $N = 3$), the coordinator can collect its W acknowledgements from the faster buffered replicas and return success to the client—all before the durable replica has finished its disk write. That disk write is already in flight and will complete shortly after, guaranteeing at least one on-disk copy. The durable write is real protection, not an afterthought; it just does not sit on the request's critical path.

The N replicas still provide a backstop—it is unlikely that all of them lose their volatile buffers in the same instant, and some datacenter servers carry a small battery to flush RAM to disk on power loss—but the designated durable write is the mechanism Dynamo actually relies on, not statistical luck.

Descendant-systems note. *Modern datacenters increasingly use NVMe flash with no moving parts. Flash brings its own wrinkle—each cell tolerates only a finite number of erase-write cycles, and an overwrite means erase-then-write—so a memory buffer that coalesces writes remains useful for both latency and device longevity.*

8.5 Summary

Chapter 8 moved from architecture into engineering: the same key-value store, tuned to be fast enough for a strict production SLA.

Table 8.1 **Chapter 8 strategies at a glance.**

Strategy	Problem it addresses	Mechanism	Trade-off
Server-side routing	Keeps the client simple	Load balancer picks a node by load; a non-owner forwards to the owner	Extra hop → higher tail latency
Smart Client (client-side)	The extra hop / tail latency	Partition-aware library routes directly to the coordinator (zero-hop)	Tight coupling to DB topology
99.9th-percentile SLA	Averages hide bad experiences	Measure and optimize the tail, e.g. 300 ms at P99.9	Costlier than chasing the mean
Write buffer	Slow disk writes at the tail	In-memory buffer + periodic flush; one replica writes durably	Small durability window on crash

What we built from first principles is, in its essentials, the system Amazon shipped as Dynamo. The chapter that follows steps back from the engineering to place that achievement in the broader sweep of the field.

References

- *DeCandia, G., et al., "Dynamo: Amazon's Highly Available Key-Value Store," ACM SOSP, 2007. §4.5 (Execution of* `get()` *and* `put()`*: client-driven vs. server-driven coordination; zero-hop routing); §6.1 (Balancing Performance and Durability: P99.9 SLA targets, write buffer, durable-write mechanism, and the latency comparison between client-driven and server-driven approaches in Table 2 of that paper).*
- *Stoica, I., et al., "Chord: A Scalable Peer-to-Peer Lookup Service for Internet Applications," ACM SIGCOMM, 2001, pp. 149–160. (Multi-hop DHT whose logarith mic hop count Dynamo's zero-hop design explicitly avoids.)*
- *Rowstron, A., and Druschel, P., "Pastry: Scalable, Distributed Object Location and Routing for Large-Scale Peer-to-Peer Systems," IFIP/ACM Middleware, 2001, pp. 329–350. (A second multi-hop DHT; cited alongside Chord in Dynamo's related-work discussion as designs whose extra forwarding hops inflate tail latency.)*

CHAPTER 9

Epilogue — The Legacy of Dynamo

You have reached the end of the architectural deep dive. You understand the Ring, the Quorum, the Gossip protocol, and conflict resolution. Everything we built up describes Amazon's original Dynamo—not to be confused with the later DynamoDB service.

Before you close the book, it is worth stepping back. Dynamo, unveiled at SOSP (the Symposium on Operating Systems Principles, one of the two most selective venues in systems research) in 2007, was more than a clever piece of engineering—it marked a turning point for the modern database industry.

Before Dynamo, scaling mostly meant buying a bigger SQL server. Dynamo's argument was that if you were willing to give up strong consistency, you could buy enormous scale in its place—in data size, in availability, and in speed. That trade-off, radical at the time, reshaped how a generation of systems was built.

9.1 The Descendants of Dynamo

Amazon never open-sourced Dynamo; it remained an internal, proprietary system. But the Dynamo design was documented in enough detail to serve as a blueprint, and engineers elsewhere built their own implementations from it. (As chapter 10 shows, so can you.)

- **Apache Cassandra**—born at Facebook. It kept Dynamo's ring and gossip for decentralised scaling but replaced the key-value "blob" with Google Bigtable's column-family storage. Facebook needed to model structured social data—friend lists, activity feeds, inbox threads—that a single opaque value cannot represent efficiently. Column families give each row a sorted, sparse set of named columns, which supports efficient prefix scans within a partition key without deserialising the entire value. Today Cassandra is a

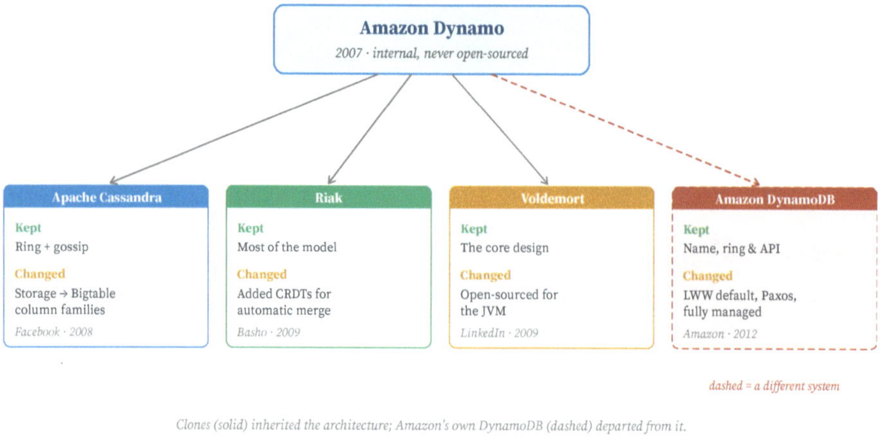

Figure 9.1 **The Family Tree of Dynamo.** Dynamo was never open-sourced, yet its design became a blueprint for clones and, later, for Amazon's own service. The clones inherited its architecture; Amazon's DynamoDB deliberately departed from it. These descendant systems all came after 2007; the original Dynamo predates them—they matter because they reveal which of Dynamo's ideas actually took hold in the industry.

standard choice for high-volume write workloads (Netflix, Apple, Uber).

- **Riak**—a near-exact implementation of the Dynamo design, written in Erlang. It pioneered using CRDTs (Conflict-Free Replicated Data Types) to make version-vector conflict resolution automatic.
- **Voldemort**—LinkedIn's open-source implementation, which powered real-time features before the company moved to Kafka and Espresso.

9.2 The Scorecard: What Stood the Test of Time?

In the years since the 2007 paper, not every idea in Dynamo aged equally. Some became defaults; others quietly fell out of favour as technology moved on and certain trade-offs stopped being necessary.

9.2.1 What Stood the Test of Time

- **Consistent hashing**—now the default way to map keys (or requests) onto a changing set of nodes with minimal reshuffling. It shows

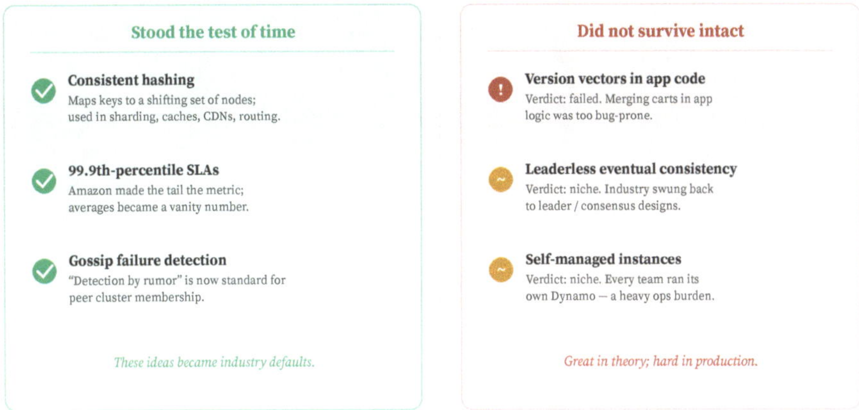

Figure 9.2 **The Scorecard.** Which of Dynamo's ideas became industry defaults, and which proved too hard in practice. Its architectural mechanics won; pushing conflict resolution into application code did not.

up in sharded data stores, caches (Memcached), CDNs, and request routing. The "ring" is everywhere.

- **The 99.9th-percentile SLA**—Dynamo's quietly most influential idea was measuring latency at the 99.9th percentile. Dynamo's target was 300 ms at the 99.9th percentile—stricter still than the now-common P99. "Average response time" is widely treated as a vanity metric; serious teams optimise the tail.
- **Gossip-based failure detection**—"detection by rumour" is now standard in clustered systems (HashiCorp Consul, Kubernetes Memberlist).

9.2.2 What Did Not Survive Intact

- **Version vectors in application code—Verdict: failed.** Asking application developers to write merge logic for conflicting shopping carts proved too difficult and bug-prone, and it slowed feature work. (The original Dynamo described these as "vector clocks"; recall that we use the more precise term, *version vectors*.)

  The gap was filled in two ways. Systems such as Riak (and later Redis Enterprise) adopted **CRDTs:** data types—counters, sets, registers—whose merge function is mathematically guaranteed to converge, so the runtime resolves conflicts automatically with no application logic at all. Other systems—CockroachDB, Spanner, etcd—took the opposite approach: **consensus-driven replication** (Raft or Paxos)

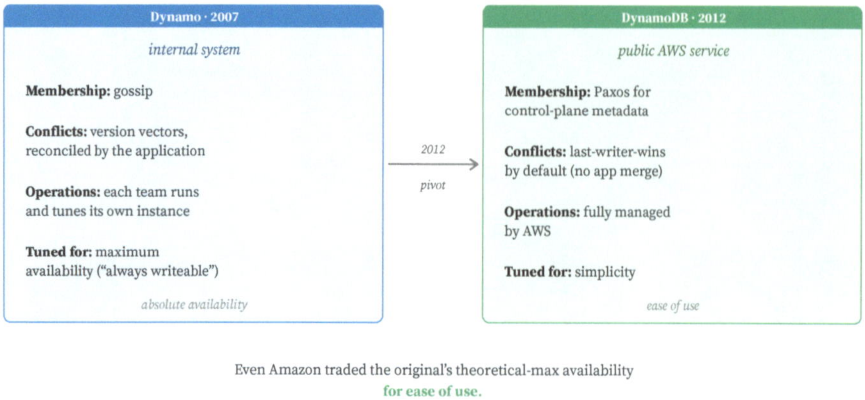

Figure 9.3 **The Pivot: Dynamo vs. DynamoDB.** The original 2007 system beside Amazon's 2012 public service that borrowed its name. Even Amazon traded maximum availability for the simplicity a cloud service demands. The points below describe DynamoDB, a post-2007 system—not the original Dynamo.

serialises writes at the source, making conflicting versions structurally impossible in the first place.

- **Pure leaderless replication—Verdict: niche.** Dynamo deliberately avoided consensus, relying on eventual consistency instead. That openness is hard to reason about and debug, so the industry largely swung back toward leader-based, consensus-driven designs (Raft, Paxos) or hybrid-clock systems like CockroachDB—trading a little latency for predictability.
- **Self-managed instances—Verdict: niche.** Dynamo was not a hosted service. Any team that wanted it had to run and tune its own instance, which demanded real operational expertise.

9.3 The Pivot: Amazon DynamoDB (2012)

When Amazon took these ideas to the public-cloud market, it did not ship the original Dynamo. In 2012 it launched **DynamoDB**—a fully managed, NoSQL key-value and document store, not a relational database—as an AWS service that shares the name and the ring but, under the hood, is a different system shaped by what a broad customer base needs rather than by what a single internal team could operate and tune. (Whether Amazon still runs the original Dynamo internally is not public; DynamoDB is a separate product, not a replacement we can observe.)

- **No version vectors.** DynamoDB's multi-region global tables default to last-writer-wins (LWW); within a single region it serialises writes through a per-partition leader. We warned earlier that LWW can silently drop concurrent writes; DynamoDB largely engineers around this—giving you tools to avoid LWW where it matters (for example, *conditional writes* let you assert that an item's version attribute equals the value you last read before overwriting it, turning a blind LWW write into a compare-and-swap that fails on a concurrent update) and keeping its internal clocks tightly synchronised—rather than solving the problem at the theoretical level. (The original Dynamo, in fact, already offered timestamp-based "last write wins" as one reconciliation option for services that wanted it.)

- **No gossip.** DynamoDB co-ordinates membership and metadata through Paxos-based consensus instead. This is not a verdict against gossip—which thrives in peer clusters elsewhere—but a fit choice: a managed, multi-tenant service wants a strongly-consistent control plane, and consensus provides exactly that.

- **The lesson.** For a public cloud service, simplicity and ease of use mattered more than squeezing out the original's last drop of theoretical availability.

9.4 If Dynamo Is the Answer, What Was the Question?

Dynamo is the right answer to one sharp question: *how do I keep writing data in a faulty environment, where nodes and networks fail?* Ask a different question, and you may need a different tool.

- **The range-query question.** Dynamo applies an MD5 hash to each key and scatters keys around the ring, so "give me all of yesterday's orders" has no efficient answer. For ordered scans you want a sorted-key store like Bigtable (built on LSM-tree storage).

- **The speed question.** You can tune Dynamo for fast reads by setting $R = 1$ and backing the storage node with an in-memory write buffer—and Amazon did exactly that for some workloads. But even at $R = 1$, a Dynamo read still pays three costs that a dedicated cache bypasses entirely: a network round-trip to the co-ordinating node (the Smart Client eliminates the forwarding hop, but not the network itself); a storage-engine lookup on the replica (an LSM-tree, or the write buffer if you are fortunate—neither is bare RAM); and a version-vector comparison to detect stale data. Redis, by contrast, is a single-process, in-memory hash table that answers `GET` from

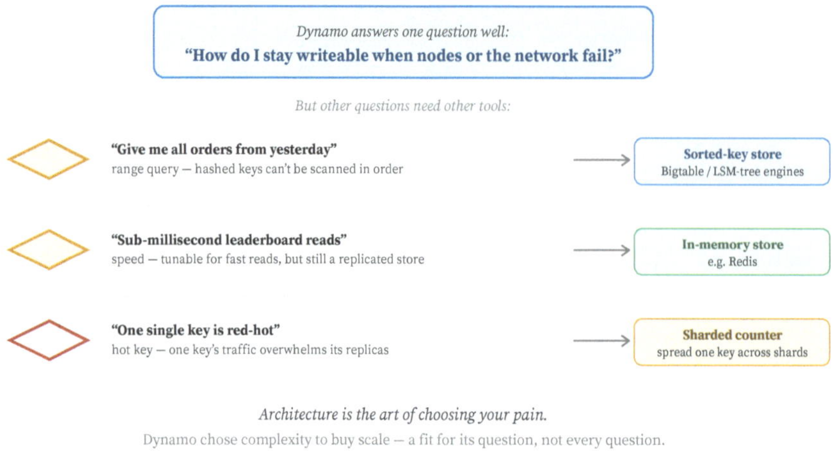

Figure 9.4 **The Right Question, the Right Tool.** Dynamo answers one question well; other questions point toward other systems. Range scans, sub-millisecond reads, and single hot keys each call for a different design.

RAM in under a hundred microseconds, with no replication round-trip on the read path and no version tracking whatsoever. For a sub-millisecond leaderboard or rate-limiter on simple, non-conflicting keys, that difference is decisive.

- **The hot-key question.** If a few keys in a partition run hot, you can split the partition finer so more servers share the load. If a single key is hot, you may need a sharded (distributed) counter: the same logical key lives in many shards, so writes stay fast and reads accumulate results across all shards.

Architecture is the discipline of choosing trade-offs. Dynamo traded **complexity** for **scale**. You now have the tools to make that choice for yourself.

References

- *DeCandia, G., et al., "Dynamo: Amazon's Highly Available Key-Value Store," ACM SOSP, 2007. The primary source for all claims about the original Dynamo design in this chapter.*
- *Lakshman, A., and Malik, P., "Cassandra: A Decentralized Structured Storage System," ACM SIGOPS Operating Systems Review, Vol. 44, No. 2, 2010 (presented at LADIS 2009). Describes Cassandra's architecture: Dynamo's ring and gossip combined with Bigtable's column-family storage model.*

- *Chang, F., et al., "Bigtable: A Distributed Storage System for Structured Data," OSDI, 2006. The source of the column-family storage model that Cassandra adopted in place of Dynamo's key-value blob.*
- *Shapiro, M., et al., "Conflict-Free Replicated Data Types," SSS (Stabilization, Safety, and Security of Distributed Systems), 2011. Formal definition of CRDTs—the approach Riak used to make conflict resolution automatic.*
- *Karger, D., et al., "Consistent Hashing and Random Trees: Distributed Caching Protocols for Relieving Hot Spots on the World Wide Web," ACM STOC, 1997. The original consistent-hashing paper; the ring Dynamo popularised is an application of this idea.*
- *Lamport, L., "Paxos Made Simple," ACM SIGACT News, Vol. 32, No. 4, 2001. The accessible presentation of the Paxos consensus algorithm used in DynamoDB's control plane and referenced as an alternative to leaderless replication.*
- *Ongaro, D., and Ousterhout, J., "In Search of an Understandable Consensus Algorithm (Extended Version)," USENIX ATC, 2014. The Raft paper; Raft is the consensus protocol now found in etcd, CockroachDB, and most modern distributed control planes.*
- *Taft, R., et al., "CockroachDB: The Resilient Geo-Distributed SQL Database," ACM SIGMOD, 2020. An example of a hybrid-clock, consensus-driven system that trades some latency for globally consistent reads—the design direction the industry moved toward after Dynamo's leaderless model proved hard to operate.*
- *Elhemali, M., et al., "Amazon DynamoDB: A Scalable, Predictably Performant, and Fully Managed NoSQL Database Service," USENIX ATC, 2022. The authoritative description of DynamoDB as it exists today—a separate product from the original 2007 Dynamo, with Paxos-based consensus and last-writer-wins as defaults.*

CHAPTER 10

Enter the Ring: Build a Dynamo that Survives Anything

You understand the design. Now prove you can build it. It is tempting to assume that once you know a key-value store inside out, writing one is easy—and at the level of boxes and arrows, it is. But implementation has a habit of surfacing the problems the design quietly hid from you. Take self-healing: the design simply says a node repairs itself, and moves on. The code makes you spell out how. Hinted handoff is event-driven—it fires the instant a recovered owner reappears—while Merkle-tree anti-entropy is a background scan you have to schedule and rate-limit yourself. Let that scan run flat out and it will starve the very requests it exists to protect. That decision is invisible from thirty thousand feet. Crossing the gap between the clean design and the messy machine is exactly what this chapter asks of you.

> **Aside: Get the Extra Advantage**
>
> Candidates who have actually built some version of their design hold a real edge over those who have only described one. Why not give yourself that edge? You may increasingly meet interviews that open with system design and then drop you straight into coding a small slice of it. More and more teams test architectural judgment directly—can you pick the right design and defend its trade-offs?—because that is the skill AI cannot replicate.

10.1 The Challenge

I challenge you to build a simplified clone of Dynamo. Do not try to build a production database—build a **Proof of Concept**.

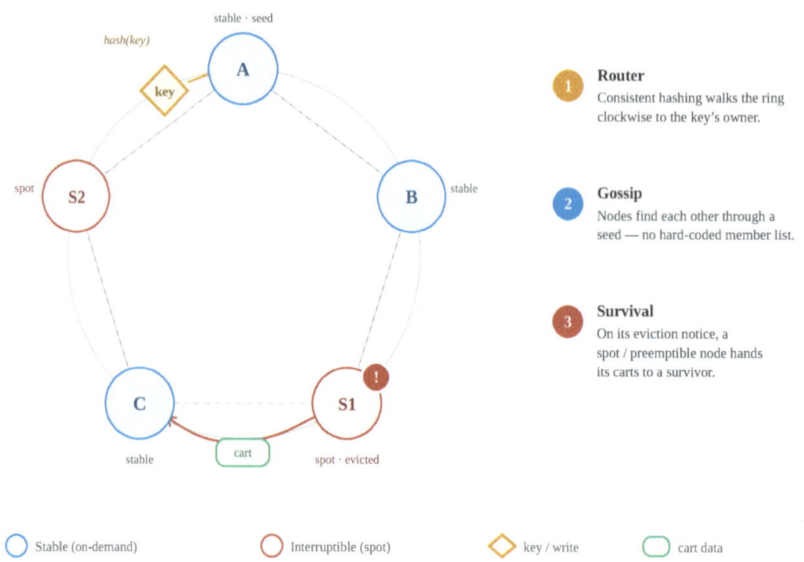

Figure 10.1 **The "Chaos Mode" Cluster.** Three stable nodes form a core; two interruptible nodes make the ring deliberately volatile. The build is three levels deep: route a write, gossip membership into existence, then survive a node being evicted.

10.1.1 The Setup: "Chaos Mode"

- **Infrastructure:** Provision three stable, on-demand instances as the Stable Core, and two interruptible instances—spot or preemptible VMs—as the Volatile Ring. Every major cloud offers both, inside the US and out: AWS, Google Cloud, Microsoft Azure, Oracle Cloud, Alibaba Cloud, and the rest.
- **Language:** Go, Python, Rust, or Node.js. Any of them works, because a Dynamo node is mostly network plumbing, not number-crunching: Go and Rust give you cheap concurrency and raw speed, Python gets you to a working prototype fastest, and Node.js's async I/O and native JSON make the request-forwarding and version-vector handling especially natural.

10.1.2 The Levels

- **Level 1—The Router.** Implement consistent hashing. Send a PUT to Node A and watch it forward the request to Node B, the correct owner.

- **Level 2—The Gossip.** Have the nodes discover one another automatically, without hard-coding the full member list. Bootstrap them from a seed—a node every other node is told about up front. Skip the seed and two nodes can each join the ring believing they are alone (a logical partition), which is exactly the failure Dynamo uses seeds to prevent.
- **Level 3—The Survival.** Wait for the cloud to reclaim an interruptible instance. It comes with a short eviction notice—about two minutes on AWS, around thirty seconds on Google Cloud and Azure. Make sure the carts on that dying node reach a survivor before it disappears.

Success metric: the system survives the churn without losing a single shopping cart.

Good luck. You now have the tools to build and reason about distributed systems of your own.

And here is the whole system on a single page—a map to keep beside you as you build:

10.2 Before You Go: The Inventory Problem

Remember, back in Chapter 1, the inventory problem for products? How does our key-value design handle it—don't we risk selling an item we don't have? If you use a pure Dynamo-style system (AP—available and partition-tolerant) for strict inventory, **you will oversell.** Here is why—and how Amazon actually handles it.

10.2.1 The "Last TV" Paradox

Dynamo is **eventually consistent**. Picture one TV left in stock, replicated on Node A and Node B:

- Node A thinks you have 1 TV left.
- Node B thinks you have 1 TV left.
- User 1 buys from Node A. Node A says "Success—inventory 0."
- *At the exact same millisecond...*
- User 2 buys from Node B. Node B says "Success—inventory 0."
- You just sold two TVs, but you only had one. This is a **write conflict**.

Neither write saw the other, so Dynamo does not silently overwrite—it keeps both as concurrent *siblings* and asks the application to reconcile them later (the machinery of Chapter 7). For a shopping cart that is a gift:

Figure 10.2 **The Dynamo Blueprint.** Amazon's highly available key-value store on one page: six mechanisms, each with its core trade-off. Keep this beside you as you build.

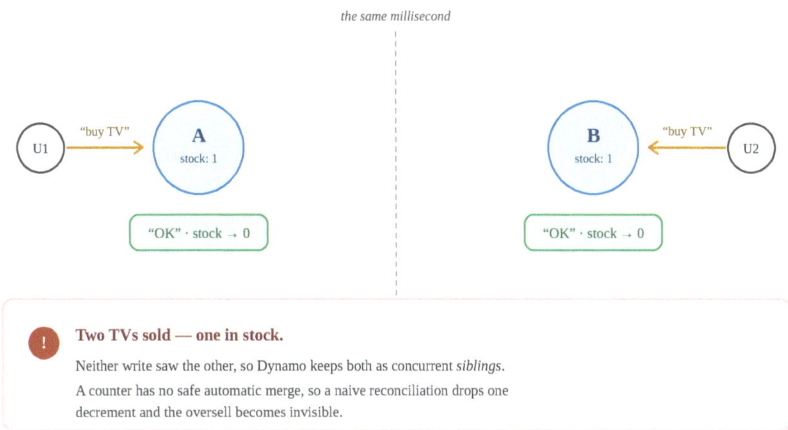

Figure 10.3 **The "Last TV" Race.** Two buyers reach two different replicas in the same instant, and both writes succeed. Dynamo keeps them as concurrent siblings; a counter has no safe automatic merge, so one decrement quietly disappears.

merge the two carts and no "add to cart" is ever lost. For a counter it is a trap, because there is no safe automatic merge of "decrement"—reconcile it naively and one of the two sales vanishes, taking your missing TV with it.

10.2.2 How Systems Handle This (Three Strategies)

The "Amazon Shopping Cart" Approach (Allow the Error)

The most important distinction in this whole book: **Dynamo was built for the shopping cart, not the inventory database.**

- **The logic:** better to let two people believe they have the TV in their cart than to block either with a "Server Busy" error.
- **The fix:** run the hard check—against a traditional ACID database or a strongly consistent service—only when the customer clicks **Place Order.**
- **The business rule:** if that check fails, show an honest error: "We're sorry, this item just sold out."

The "Compensating Transaction" Approach (Sell Now, Settle Later)

Sometimes a high-speed system simply accepts the risk of overselling.

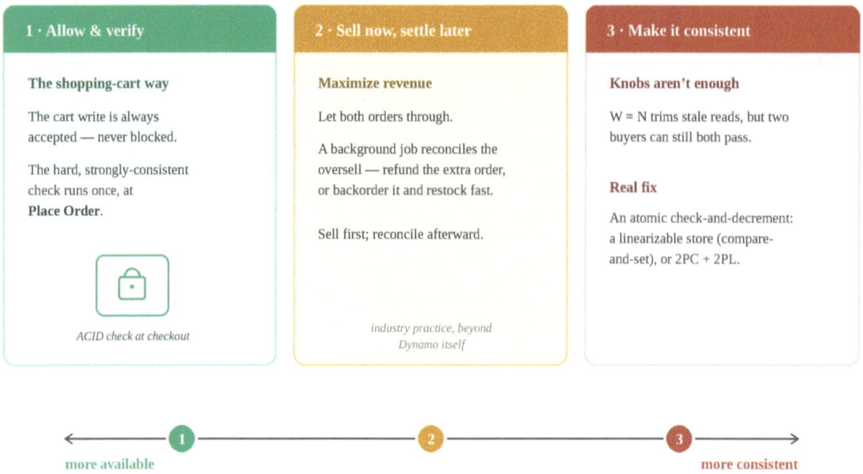

Figure 10.4 **Three Ways to Handle the Oversell.** Allow-and-verify, sell-now-settle-later, and make-it-consistent trade availability for correctness in that order. Only the data that truly cannot oversell pays the availability cost; carts stay always-writable.

- **The logic:** let both orders through. Maximize revenue.
- **The fix:** a background process notices stock has gone negative and runs a *compensating transaction*—refund the extra order, or backorder it and replenish stock quickly so it still ships.
- **Why:** for Amazon, selling 100,000 items in a flash on Prime Day is worth settling up with a handful of customers afterward.

A compensating transaction is one step of a saga—a sequence of small local transactions, each paired with an "undo," that keeps several services in agreement without holding one big distributed lock. It is how teams live with eventual consistency at the application layer; Dynamo itself does not prescribe it.

The "Consistency" Approach (Why a Quorum Isn't Enough)

It is tempting to reach for the quorum knobs and call it solved: set $W = N$ so every replica must acknowledge a write. That tightens things, but it does not stop the oversell. Two buyers can still read "one left" at the same instant and both pass their check—quorum tuning governs how stale a single read is, not whether two operations may interleave. And because Dynamo uses a sloppy quorum with hinted handoff, even $W = N$ can be acknowledged by a temporary stand-in rather than a true owner, so the guarantee is *tighter*, not *linearizable* (the same gap we drew in Chapter 5).

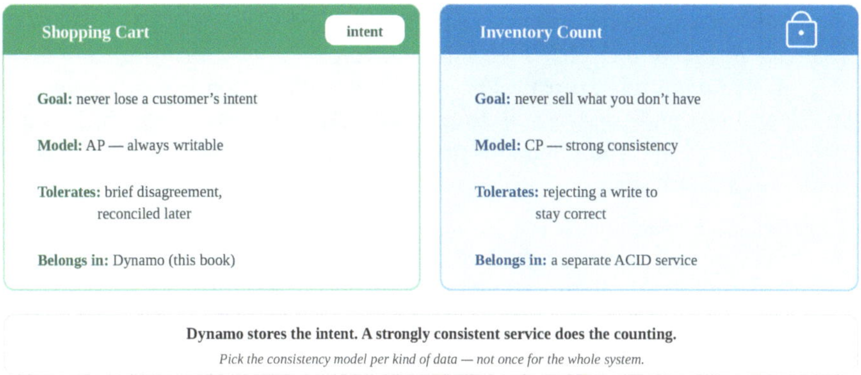

Figure 10.5 **Not All Data Is Equal.** A cart optimizes for never losing intent; an inventory count optimizes for never overselling. They want opposite guarantees, so they belong in different systems.

What the oversell really needs is an **atomic, isolated check-and-decrement**—read the count, and only if it is positive commit the decrement, with no one slipping in between. Two tools deliver that:

- A linearizable store with a conditional (compare-and-set) write—the count lives in one consistent place that applies decrements in order.
- Full distributed transactions—**two-phase commit** to make the change atomic across participants, and **two-phase locking** (or an equivalent serializable isolation) to stop the two buyers from interleaving.

None of that is Dynamo's job. When you truly cannot oversell, don't bend Dynamo into the wrong shape—put the count in a system built for it.

This is the key lesson of system design: **not all data is equal.**

- Shopping carts need **high availability**—never lose a customer's intent.
- Inventory counts need **strong consistency**—never sell what you don't have.

In this book we built the shopping cart—the system that must never say "Service Unavailable." We hand the strict counting to a different, strongly consistent service downstream. Build that, survive the churn, and you will have done more than read about Dynamo: you will have lived inside its trade-offs.

References

- *Haerder, T., and Reuter, A., "Principles of Transaction-Oriented Database Recovery," ACM Computing Surveys, Vol. 15, No. 4, 1983. The paper that coined the ACID acronym and gave formal definitions to Atomicity, Consistency, Isolation, and Durability—the guarantees the inventory counter needs but Dynamo deliberately does not provide.*
- *Eswaran, K. P., Gray, J., Lorie, R., and Traiger, I., "The Notions of Consistency and Predicate Locks in a Database System," Communications of the ACM, Vol. 19, No. 11, 1976. The original two-phase locking (2PL) paper; the mechanism that prevents two concurrent buyers from interleaving their check-and-decrement.*
- *Gray, J., "Notes on Database Operating Systems," in Operating Systems: An Advanced Course, Lecture Notes in Computer Science, Vol. 60, Springer, 1978. The canonical reference for two-phase commit (2PC) as a protocol for making a write atomic across multiple participants—one of the two tools cited in §10.2 for strict inventory.*
- *Garcia-Molina, H., and Salem, K., "Sagas," ACM SIGMOD, 1987. Introduces the saga pattern: a sequence of local transactions each paired with a compensating "undo" step. The compensating-transaction approach in §10.2 is a direct application of this idea at the application layer.*
- *Herlihy, M., and Wing, J., "Linearizability: A Correctness Condition for Concurrent Objects," ACM Transactions on Programming Languages and Systems, Vol. 12, No. 3, 1990. Formal definition of linearizability—the guarantee a compare-and-set store must provide so that decrements are applied in order with no interleaving.*
- *Gilbert, S., and Lynch, N., "Brewer's Conjecture and the Feasibility of Consistent, Available, Partition-Tolerant Web Services," ACM SIGACT News, Vol. 33, No. 2, 2002. The formal proof of the CAP theorem that underlies this chapter's central lesson: a shopping cart and an inventory counter want opposite points in the AP/CP trade-off space, so they belong in different systems.*
- *Kleppmann, M., Designing Data-Intensive Applications, O'Reilly, 2017. Chapters 7 and 9 cover transactions, isolation levels, 2PC, linearizability, and consistency models in depth—the best single resource for engineers who want to go deeper on the database and distributed-systems topics introduced in this chapter.*

APPENDICES

APPENDIX A

Merkle Trees: A Data-Structure Primer

In the main text we used Merkle trees as a tool: a black box that lets two replicas discover their differences cheaply. A system-design book can usually get away with that. But a careful reader quickly hits a question the black box cannot answer—*"if a leaf only stores a hash of a value, how does anyone know which key it belongs to?"* That question deserves a real answer, because the way you resolve it is exactly the difference between a Merkle tree that works and one that quietly breaks. This appendix teaches the structure properly, the way you would meet it in a data-structures course, using the same shopping-cart, key, and value vocabulary as the rest of the book.

A.1 The Problem It Solves

Two machines each hold a large set of key–value pairs that are *supposed* to be identical—two replicas of the same shopping-cart data, say, ten million carts, a hundred gigabytes each. After a network hiccup some keys fell out of sync. How do they identify and repair only the differing keys, without shipping the whole dataset over the wire?

The naive options are both bad. Comparing key by key means streaming everything across the network. Comparing a single hash of the *whole* dataset tells you only *that* something differs, never *where*. A Merkle tree is the structure that lives between those two extremes: a hierarchy of hashes that lets you zoom in on differences with a logarithmic number of comparisons.

A.2 The Building Block: A Hash Function

A hash function takes any input and returns a fixed-size fingerprint—for example a 128-bit number. The properties we rely on:

- **Deterministic.** The same input always yields the same fingerprint. Two replicas that hold identical data compute identical hashes.
- **Fixed-size.** A one-byte value and a one-megabyte value both hash to, say, 128 bits. That is why a hash can stand in for arbitrarily large data in a comparison.
- **Avalanche.** Change a single byte of the input and roughly half the output bits flip. A stale cart and a fresh cart produce wildly different fingerprints, so differences are never missed.
- **Collision-resistant (for the strong variants).** It is computationally infeasible to find two different inputs with the same fingerprint.

> **Aside: How Strong a Hash Do You Actually Need?**
>
> For anti-entropy the threat is **accidental** drift, not a malicious adversary crafting collisions, so even a fast, non-cryptographic hash is usually enough—Dynamo applies MD5 to keys for placement, and a similar non-cryptographic hash suffices for Merkle comparisons. Tamper-evident contexts (Git, Bitcoin) do need a cryptographic hash such as SHA-256, because an attacker who can craft a collision can make a corrupt commit look clean.

A.3 Anatomy of a Merkle Tree

A Merkle tree (or hash tree) is a binary tree built bottom-up out of hashes:

- **Leaves** sit at the bottom. Each leaf holds the hash of the (key, value) pairs in one small range of the key space.
- **Internal nodes** each hold the hash of their two children's hashes—a hash of hashes.
- **The root** is a single hash that fingerprints the entire range. If two replicas' roots match, every leaf beneath them matches, and the replicas are in sync.

The defining property: **every node summarizes everything beneath it.** Change any key or value at the very bottom and its leaf hash changes, which changes its parent, and so on up to the root. A single difference anywhere in the dataset—a modified value, a deleted key, an added entry—is guaranteed to surface as a mismatch at the root.

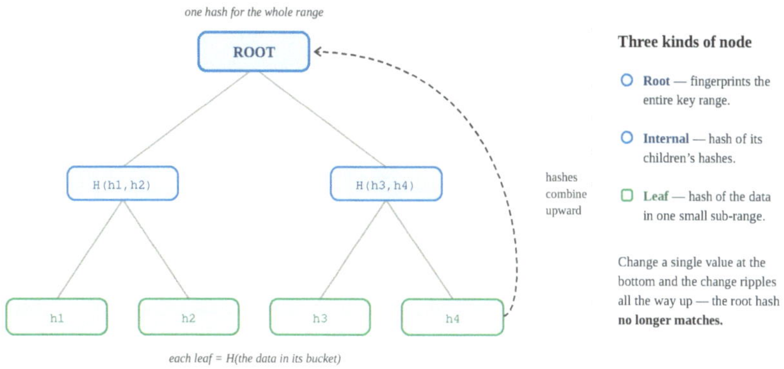

Figure A.1 **Anatomy of a Merkle Tree.** Leaves hash data; internal nodes hash their children; the root fingerprints the whole range. Any change at the bottom ripples all the way up to the root.

A.4 Building One from Shopping-Cart Data

Here is the part that answers the reader's question—and it hinges on a single design decision: **the leaves are defined by key range, not by individual keys.**

To build the tree over a range of carts:

- **Carve the key range into a fixed number of buckets.** Decide up front, independent of the data, that the range splits into (say) four equal sub-ranges B0–B3. This split is chosen by the range boundaries alone; it does not change when keys are added or removed.
- **Hash each bucket's contents into a leaf.** A leaf's hash is computed over all the *(key, value)* pairs whose keys fall in that bucket, serialised in a canonical order (sorted by key, so both replicas produce the same byte sequence). **Both the key and the value are included**: including the key means that a rename—the same value moving to a different key—is detected as a difference; including the value means that a modified cart is detected even if its key is unchanged. The leaf for an *empty* bucket gets a canonical "empty hash"—a fixed, well-known value that both replicas agree on.
- **Combine upward to the root.** Hash adjacent leaf hashes into parents, parents into grandparents, until a single root remains.

So the honest, layered answer to *"which key is this leaf?"* is: a leaf's **position** in the tree identifies the key sub-range it represents, and its **hash** is

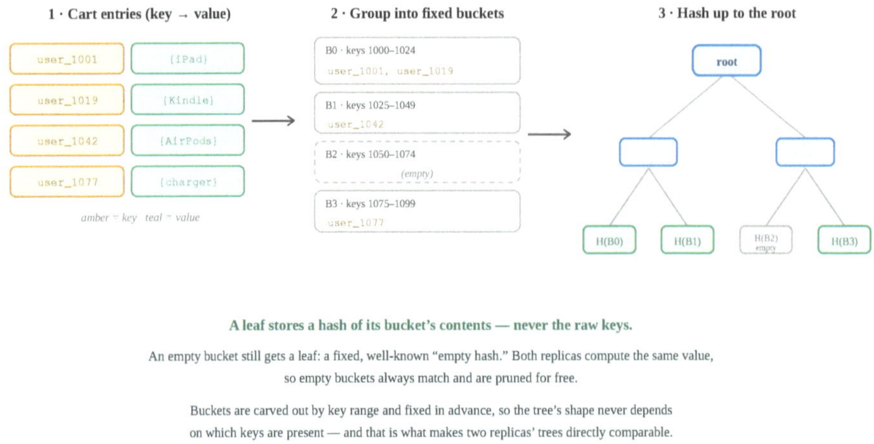

Figure A.2 **Building the Tree from Carts.** Entries are grouped into fixed key-range buckets; each bucket is hashed into a leaf, then hashes combine to a root. The empty bucket B2 still gets a leaf—a canonical "empty hash"—so both replicas always produce identically shaped trees.

derived from every (key, value) pair whose key falls in that range. There is no single "key for a leaf"—but every key and every value that falls in the leaf's range contributes to its hash.

A.5 The Crucial Choice: Fix Leaf Positions by Range, Not by Data

Why bucket by range at all—why not give every key its own leaf? The subtle trap is *not* granularity; it is letting the **data** decide where leaves sit. If you take the keys that happen to be present and build a tree around them, two replicas that differ by even one key will produce trees with different shapes—and different-shaped trees cannot be compared position by position.

What actually makes two trees comparable is that leaf positions are fixed **in advance by the key space**, independent of which keys exist. Given that, an empty slot on one replica and a populated slot on the other occupy the *same* position in the tree, so a comparison finds the discrepancy immediately.

Data-independence can be reached two ways, and they differ *only* in how fine the fixed slots are. One extreme gives every **possible** key its own slot—a **sparse Merkle tree**—which lines up perfectly but produces an as-

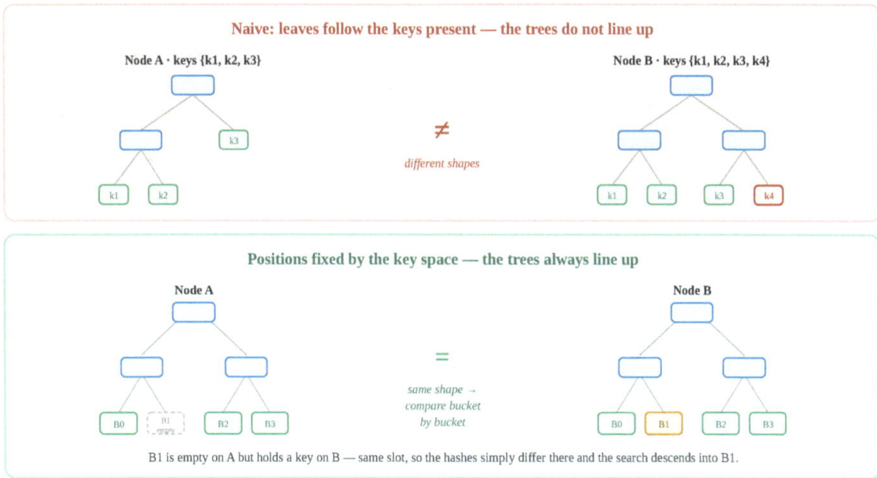

Figure A.3 **Data-Dependent vs. Data-Independent Leaf Positions.** Leaves placed by the keys that happen to be present diverge in shape and cannot be aligned; positions fixed by the key space always produce identically shaped trees that can be compared bucket by bucket.

tronomically large tree for wide key spaces. The practical middle ground is **range buckets**: decide on a fixed number of contiguous key sub-ranges and assign one leaf to each. That is the approach Dynamo uses, and it is what Chapter 6 calls a "fixed partition" (see Chapter 6).

So which key is the "root"? None.

A common first instinct is to picture a binary *search* tree with some key (say 50) at the root and keys sorting into place. That is not a Merkle tree. Here, "50" is a **range boundary**—the midpoint that splits the key space in two. No individual key owns any node; nodes own *ranges*.

A.6 Comparing Two Trees: The Diff Walk

With identically shaped trees, synchronizing two replicas is a top-down walk:

- **Compare roots.** If they match, the replicas are identical and you are done—one hash exchanged for the whole dataset. If not, descend.
- **Compare children.** For each child position, equal hashes mean that entire subtree is identical—prune it, never look inside. Unequal hashes mark the half that contains a difference.
- **Recurse to the leaves.** Keep splitting the disagreement until you reach the specific bucket(s) whose leaf hashes differ.

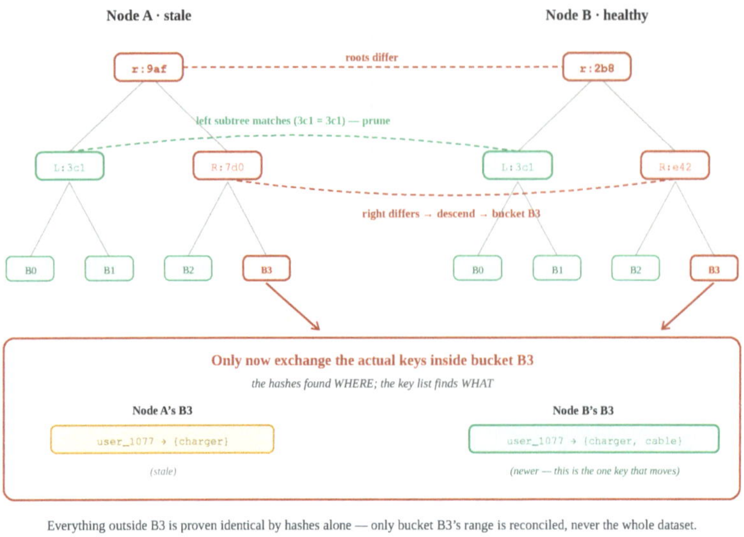

Figure A.4 **The Diff Walk, Then Bucket Reconciliation.** Hashes localize the disagreement to one leaf (B3); matching subtrees are pruned untouched. Only that bucket's range is reconciled—here, the single stale `user_1077` key whose cart is missing a cable.

- **Only then reconcile the differing bucket.** Inside each differing leaf—and only there—the nodes reconcile the keys in that bucket's range, exchanging keys and version metadata to bring the two replicas into agreement.

The payoff: everything outside the differing leaves is proven identical by a handful of tiny hash comparisons. For a sparse difference, the work is roughly proportional to the number of differing leaves times the tree depth—far less than scanning every key.

A.7 Cost: When Merkle Trees Win (and When They Don't)

Merkle trees are tuned for **sparse** differences—a needle in a haystack. Each difference costs one root-to-leaf path of hash comparisons, so a few stray carts are found almost for free. But the back-and-forth hash exchange has its own overhead on top of whatever data finally moves.

Past a crossover point (very roughly a quarter of the data differing, depending on tree shape and round-trip costs), you are no longer hunting a needle—you have two different haystacks, and streaming the entire dataset is cheaper than walking the tree.

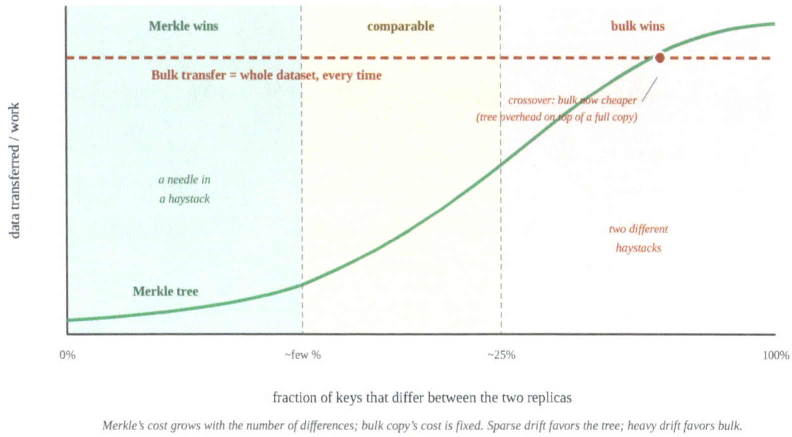

Figure A.5 **The Cost Trade-Off.** Merkle cost rises with the number of differences; bulk transfer is a fixed ceiling. Sparse drift favors the tree; heavy drift favors a full copy.

Aside: Bounded Depth, Bounded Overhead

A tree with one leaf per **possible** key (a full sparse tree) has astronomically many leaves, so practical systems cap the tree depth instead. Cassandra, a direct Dynamo descendant, uses a fixed depth of 15 during repair.

Why 15? A binary tree of depth 15 has $2^{15} = 32\,768$ leaf buckets. Each comparison round traverses one level, so localising a disagreement from root to leaf takes at most 15 network round-trips—small enough to be negligible compared with the data transfer that follows.

Why "$\sim$30 partitions per leaf"? That figure is not universal; it depends on how many partitions the repaired range contains. If a token range holds roughly one million partitions, dividing by $2^{15} = 32\,768$ leaves gives about 30 partitions per bucket. On smaller deployments each bucket covers fewer; on a very large cluster with tens of millions of partitions, each bucket covers more. Depth 15 was chosen so that the comparison overhead is cheap across the whole plausible range of cluster sizes, while still localising disagreements to a manageable key sub-range.

Note: the Dynamo paper (§4.7) describes Merkle anti-entropy but does not pin down leaf granularity; the depth-15 design is Cassandra's production implementation, included here as practical context from a direct

> *descendant.*

A.8 Implementation Notes and Practical Variations

- **Fan-out is tunable.** We drew binary trees for teaching, but real systems often use wider fan-out (more children per node) to trade a shallower tree and fewer network round-trips against larger messages per exchange.
- **Granularity is a knob.** Finer buckets localize differences more precisely but make a bigger tree; coarser buckets mean smaller trees but more keys to exchange once a bucket mismatches. Systems pick the crossover that minimizes total bytes moved in their typical failure scenarios.
- **Build on a frozen snapshot.** As covered in Chapter 6, the tree is computed over an immutable point-in-time snapshot so that live writes do not change the hashes mid-comparison.
- **One tree per ring slice.** In Dynamo, each node keeps a separate Merkle tree for each portion of the consistent-hash ring it is responsible for (called a "virtual node" or "token range"). Two nodes only compare trees for the ring slices they share—so before a single leaf is examined, both sides are guaranteed to be talking about the same arc of the ring and the same span of the key space.

A.9 Where You'll Meet Merkle Trees Again

The same structure, with the tamper-evidence property doing the heavy lifting, shows up well beyond replica repair:

- **Git** names every commit by the root hash of a Merkle tree over the repository's files and directories; identical subtrees are stored once.
- **Bitcoin and other blockchains** put a Merkle root of all transactions in each block header, so a light client can verify a transaction's inclusion with a short path of hashes rather than the whole block.
- **IPFS and content-addressed stores** address data by its hash and deduplicate shared subtrees.
- **ZFS and other filesystems** checksum blocks in a hash tree to detect silent corruption on disk.
- **Cassandra**—a direct Dynamo descendant—builds exactly the range-bucketed repair trees described here for its anti-entropy repair.

A.10 Summary

A Merkle tree turns "compare two large datasets" into "compare two small hashes, then zoom in only where they disagree." The single design decision that makes it work for replica repair is to define leaf positions by **key range rather than by the keys present**—that gives both replicas identically shaped trees they can compare position by position, regardless of what data is or is not stored in each slot.

References

[1] Merkle, R. C. (1988). A digital signature based on a conventional encryption function. In *Advances in Cryptology—CRYPTO '87*, Lecture Notes in Computer Science vol. 293, pp. 369–378. Springer. (The foundational paper establishing the hash-tree construction; the underlying technique appears in Merkle's 1979 Stanford Ph.D. dissertation.)

[2] DeCandia, G., Hastorun, D., Jampani, M., Kakulapati, G., Lakshman, A., Pilchin, A., Sivasubramanian, S., Vosshall, P., & Vogels, W. (2007). Dynamo: Amazon's highly available key-value store. In *Proc. 21st ACM Symposium on Operating Systems Principles (SOSP '07)*, pp. 205–220. ACM. (§4.7 describes the Merkle-tree anti-entropy protocol that Chapter 6 of this book covers.)

[3] Lakshman, A., & Malik, P. (2010). Cassandra: A decentralized structured storage system. *ACM SIGOPS Operating Systems Review*, 44(2), 35–40. (Describes Cassandra's inheritance of Dynamo's anti-entropy approach, including the bounded-depth Merkle tree used in repair.)

APPENDIX **B**

Logical Time: From Lamport Clocks to Version Vectors

In Chapter 7 we *used* version vectors to detect conflicting shopping carts. This appendix steps back and builds the whole family of logical clocks from first principles, so you can re-derive them yourself rather than memorize the result. We move in three steps: the **happens-before** relation that defines what "order" even means without a shared clock; **Lamport clocks**, which give a usable order but cannot see concurrency; and **vector clocks** / **version vectors**, which can. This is foundational distributed-systems theory; the 2007 Dynamo paper cites it rather than deriving it, and what Dynamo actually ships is the version-vector specialization.

B.1 Why We Need Logical Clocks

Every machine has a quartz clock, and protocols like NTP (Network Time Protocol, which continuously adjusts each node's clock by comparing it against reference servers) keep them roughly aligned. But "roughly" is the problem. Clocks drift; synchronization only *bounds* the gap, it never closes it. Across a wide-area system the skew can reach tens of milliseconds—enough to reorder events that happened a hair apart.

The deeper point is that we usually do not need to know *what time it is*. We need to know *what happened before what*—which write caused which, and which writes were independent. That is a question about **causality**, and a wall clock answers a different question. When we press a wall clock into service to answer a causal question, we get the failure shown in Figure B.1.

B.2 The Happens-Before Relation

Leslie Lamport's 1978 insight was to define order without clocks at all, using only what a system can actually observe: local sequence and mes-

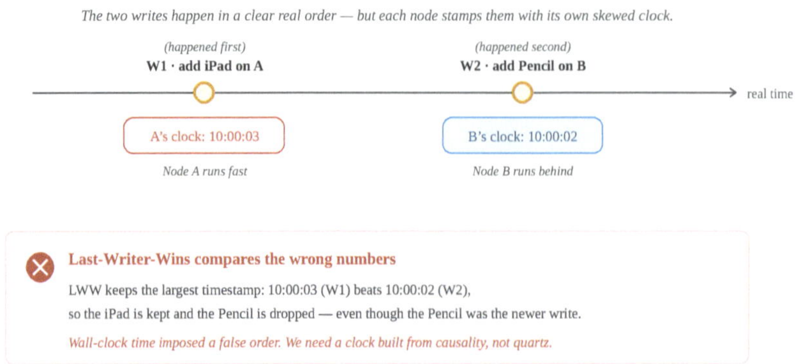

Figure B.1 **Why Wall Clocks Lie.** Two writes with a clear real order get stamped by skewed node clocks, so Last-Writer-Wins keeps the older one. A logical clock orders events by causality instead of quartz.

sages. He defined the **happens-before** relation, written $\rightarrow$, by three rules:

- If a and b happen in the **same process** and a comes before b, then $a \rightarrow b$.
- If a is the **sending** of a message and b is its **receipt**, then $a \rightarrow b$.
- If $a \rightarrow b$ and $b \rightarrow c$, then $a \rightarrow c$ (*transitivity*).

Two events are **concurrent** (written $a \parallel b$) when *neither* $a \rightarrow b$ nor $b \rightarrow a$ holds—there is no chain of messages connecting them in either direction. The crucial consequence: $\rightarrow$ is only a **partial** order. Some pairs of events are genuinely unordered, and no honest clock can invent an order for them.

B.3 Lamport Clocks: One Counter

A Lamport clock is the simplest logical clock: a single integer per process, updated by two rules.

> **Aside: Algorithm — Lamport Clock**
>
> Each process keeps a counter L, starting at 0. Before timestamping a local event or a send, it increments L by 1. Every message carries the sender's L. On receiving a message with value t, the process sets $L = \max(L,\ t) + 1$; that becomes the receive event's timestamp.

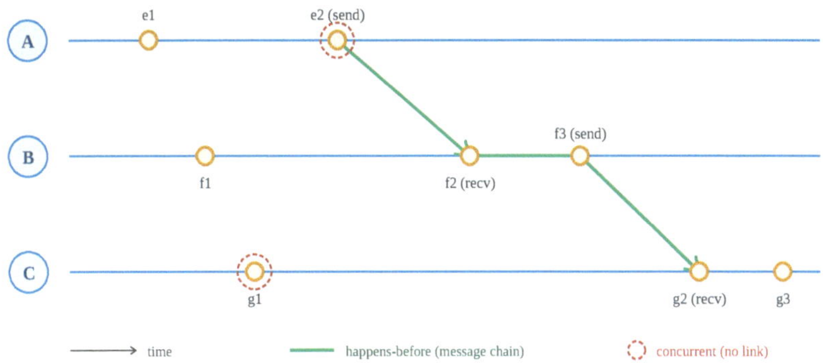

Figure B.2 **The Happens-Before Relation.** A chain of messages links e_2 to g_2, so $e_2 \to g_2$. No chain links e_2 and g_1, so they are concurrent. "Happens-before" is a partial order—some events simply have no order.

Applying this to our three nodes gives the numbers in Figure B.3. The clock keeps one promise: **if** $a \to b$ **then** $L(a) < L(b)$. A cause always has a smaller stamp than its effect. By breaking ties with a fixed node ordering, we can even turn this into a *total* order over all events—handy when you just need *some* consistent sequence.

But there is a catch, and it is the whole reason version vectors exist. The promise runs **one way only**. A smaller stamp does *not* prove a causal link. In the figure, $g_1 = 1$ and $e_2 = 2$, so the numbers suggest g_1 came "before" e_2—yet no message connects them. They are concurrent, and the Lamport clock cannot tell you so.

B.4 Vector Clocks: One Counter per Process

Vector clocks fix the blind spot by remembering *more*. Instead of one number, each process carries a vector with one entry per process.

> **Aside: Algorithm — Vector Clock (N Processes)**
>
> Each process i keeps a vector V of length N, all zeros. Before a local event or a send at i, it increments its own entry: $V[i] = V[i] + 1$. Messages carry the sender's whole vector. On receiving a vector W at process i, set $V[k] = \max(V[k], W[k])$ for every k, then increment $V[i]$. Compare two vectors entry by entry: $V \leq W$ when $V[k] \leq W[k]$ for all k; and $V < W$ when $V \leq W$ and $V \neq W$.

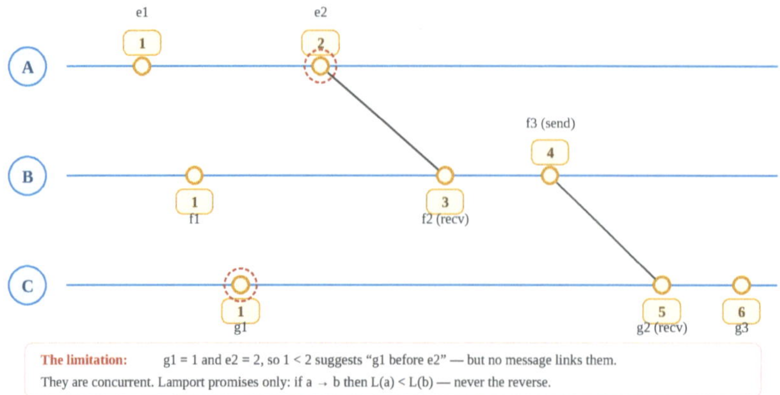

Figure B.3 **Lamport Clocks and Their Limit.** One counter per process gives every event a number, but concurrent events (g_1, e_2) still receive an order. A smaller Lamport stamp does not prove "happened-before."

Now the guarantee runs **both ways:** $a \to b$ exactly when $V(a) < V(b)$. And when neither vector is less than the other, the events are **concurrent**—detectable at last. In Figure B.4, $e_2 = [2, 0, 0]$ and $g_1 = [0, 0, 1]$ are incomparable (each leads on a different entry), so the system correctly reports them as concurrent—precisely the pair Lamport mis-ordered.

The price is size: a vector clock carries one entry per process, so in a 500-node system every stamp has 500 entries. That cost is exactly what the next specialization trims down.

B.5 Version Vectors: One Entry per Replica

A **version vector** is a vector clock pointed at a narrower target: the update history of a single replicated *object*, rather than every event in the system. Each entry counts the updates contributed by one *replica,* and the comparison rule is identical to Chapter 7's rules of dominance:

- X is a **descendant** of Y if X's count is $\geq Y$'s at every entry (a missing entry counts as 0) and strictly greater at one—X already contains Y.
- If each leads on some entry, they are **concurrent siblings**—the `[A:3]` vs. `[A:2, B:1]` case from the cart walkthrough.

Why is this so much cheaper than a full vector clock? Because an entry appears only for a replica that has actually *coordinated a write* to *this object.* In normal operation that is just one of the top-N preference-list nodes, so the vector stays tiny—which is exactly why Dynamo only rarely needs the clock truncation of Chapter 7.

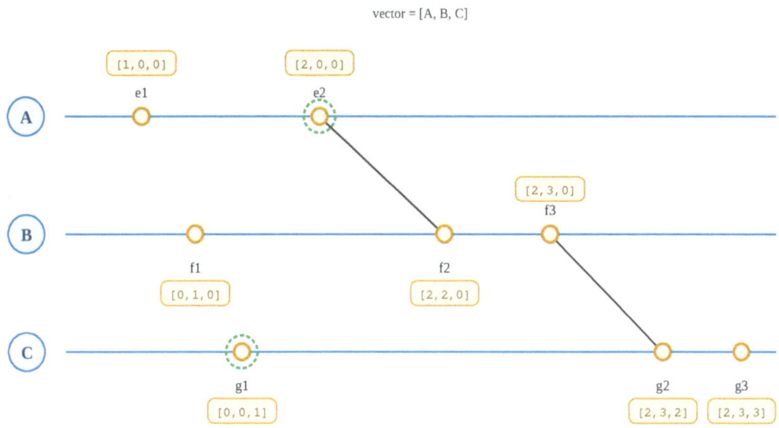

Figure B.4 **Vector Clocks Detect Concurrency.** One counter per process, merged on every message. e_2 and g_1 are now incomparable, so the system sees them as concurrent—the distinction Lamport clocks cannot make.

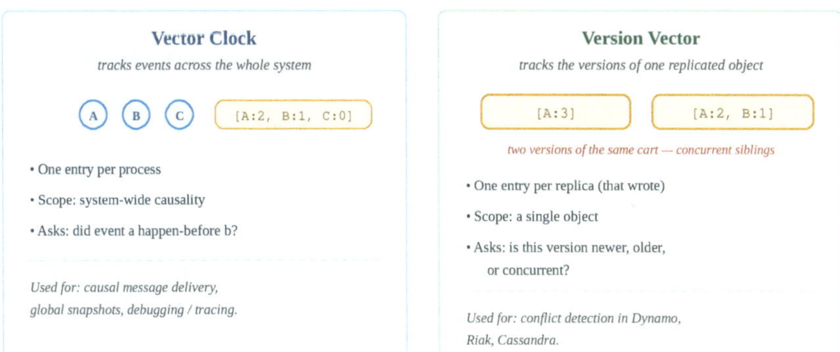

Figure B.5 **Vector Clock vs. Version Vector.** Same update rules and the same partial-order test—different scope. A vector clock tracks events across the whole system; a version vector tracks the versions of one replicated object.

Table B.1 Vector clock vs. version vector—same math, different scope.

Aspect	Vector Clock	Version Vector
Tracks	Events across processes	Versions of one object
One entry per	Process	Replica that coordinated a write
Scope	System-wide causality	A single object
Core question	Did event a happen-before b?	Is this version newer, older, or concurrent?
Typical setting	Causal delivery, snapshots, tracing	Replicated-storage conflict detection
Examples	Distributed algorithms, debuggers	Dynamo, Riak, Cassandra

Aside: A Short History (and a Twist)

The pieces arrived in an order that may surprise you.
1978: Lamport formalizes happens-before and the scalar logical clock.
1983: Parker et al. introduce *version vectors* to detect inconsistency among replicas.
1988: Fidge and Mattern, independently, formalize *vector clocks* and establish their partial-order properties.
So although we teach version vectors as a *specialization* of vector clocks, historically the version vector came **first**—by about five years. The mechanism is shared; the names reflect two communities (systems theory vs. storage) that arrived at the same idea from different doors.

B.6 When to Use Which

The two structures share the same arithmetic; what differs is what each one is counting and why. A simple rule of thumb: ordering events across a whole system calls for a vector clock; tracking the versions of one replicated object calls for a version vector.

In short: **events across the system → vector clock; versions of one object → version vector.**

B.7 The Payoff: Why Last-Writer-Wins Needs a Wall Clock

This appendix's thread ties directly back to Chapter 7's discussion of LWW. Every logical clock gives only a **partial** order, and concurrent versions are, by definition, **incomparable**—there is no "larger" one. So the moment two writes are concurrent, a logical clock has nothing left to say.

Yet a policy like Last-Writer-Wins *must* pick a single winner. To do that it needs a **total** order—and a logical clock cannot supply one without resorting to an arbitrary tie-break. That is why LWW reaches for **physical wall-clock time**: it is a convenient total order. The catch is the one raised in Chapter 7—physical time is skewed, so an older write can carry the larger timestamp and overwrite a genuinely newer one.

This is the clean division of labor in Dynamo. A **version vector** answers the question logical clocks *can* answer—"are these two versions ordered, or concurrent?" Resolving the concurrent case is a separate decision: hand the siblings to the application to *merge* (the cart), or, for overwrite-friendly data with no merge semantics, fall back to physical-timestamp LWW (the session store). Logical time detects the conflict; only a total order can break it—and the only total order on hand is the wall clock we started by distrusting.

References

[1] Lamport, L. (1978). Time, clocks, and the ordering of events in a distributed system. *Communications of the ACM*, 21(7), 558–565. (The paper that defines the happens-before relation and the scalar logical clock; Sections B.2 and B.3 of this appendix are drawn directly from it.)

[2] Parker, D. S., Popek, G. J., Rudisin, G., Stoughton, A., Walker, B., Walton, E., Chow, J., Edwards, D., Kiser, S., & Kline, C. (1983). Detection of mutual inconsistency in distributed systems. *IEEE Transactions on Software Engineering*, 9(3), 240–247. (Introduced version vectors—five years before vector clocks were formalised—to detect replica inconsistency in storage systems.)

[3] Fidge, C. J. (1988). Timestamps in message-passing systems that preserve the partial ordering. In *Proc. 11th Australian Computer Science Conference (ACSC '88)*, pp. 56–66. (One of the two independent formalisations of vector clocks; establishes the bidirectional happens-before equivalence that Section B.4 relies on.)

[4] Mattern, F. (1988). Virtual time and global states of distributed systems. In *Parallel and Distributed Algorithms*, pp. 215–226. North-

Holland. (The simultaneous and independent formalisation of vector clocks; together with Fidge [3] it is the canonical reference.)

[5] DeCandia, G., Hastorun, D., Jampani, M., Kakulapati, G., Lakshman, A., Pilchin, A., Sivasubramanian, S., Vosshall, P., & Vogels, W. (2007). Dynamo: Amazon's highly available key-value store. In *Proc. 21st ACM Symposium on Operating Systems Principles (SOSP '07)*, pp. 205–220. ACM. (Sections 4.4 and 4.5 describe Dynamo's version-vector implementation—called "vector clock" in the paper—along with the clock-truncation scheme of Chapter 7.)

www.ingramcontent.com/pod-product-compliance
Lightning Source LLC
LaVergne TN
LVHW070936210926
848482LV00003B/251
* 9 7 9 8 9 9 6 7 6 5 4 2 3 *